THE 24 HOUR BUSINESS PLAN

THE
24 HOUR BUSINESS PLAN

*A Step-by-Step Guide to Producing
a Tailor-Made Business Plan in
24 Working Hours*

RON JOHNSON

RANDOM HOUSE

BUSINESS BOOKS

This edition first published in the United Kingdom by Century Ltd
Random House, 20 Vauxhall Bridge Road, London SW1V 2SA

Random House Australia (Pty) Limited
20 Alfred Street, Milsons Point
Sydney, New South Wales 2061, Australia

Random House New Zealand Limited
18 Poland Road, Glenfield
Auckland 10, New Zealand

Random House South Africa (Pty) Limited
Endulini, 5a Jubilee Road, Parktown 2193, South Africa

Random House UK Limited Reg. No. 954009

Papers used by Random House UK Limited are natural, recyclable products made from wood grown in sustainable forests. The manufacturing processes conform to the environmental regulations of the country of origin.

ISBN 0 7126 7779 8

Typeset by SX Composing DTP, Rayleigh, Essex
Printed and bound in Great Britain by Butler & Tanner Ltd, Frome, Somerset

Companies, institutions and other organizations wishing to make bulk purchases of any business books published by Random House should contact their local bookstore or Random House direct:

Special Sales Director
Random House, 20 Vauxhall Bridge Road, London SW1V 2SA

Tel 020 7840 8470   Fax 020 7828 6681

Contents

Part Five

FINANCIAL STRATEGY

Part Six

PUTTING IT TOGETHER

Part Seven

THE BUSINESS PLAN

FOREWORD

This book takes you step by step through the complex process of drawing up a credible business plan for a three-year period. Some firms plan five, seven or even more years ahead, but many firms do little serious forward planning and if you are new to this activity, three years is not a bad start.

The book does *not* set out to teach you how to run your business, or manage your accounts, sales, production or distribution. It assumes you can do that already. However, many managers are not all that familiar with the financial terms used in a business plan and I have attempted to explain most of these, when they occur, in simple terms.

If you have all the information at your fingertips, it really does take only about 24 hours to write a business plan for a simple business. However, if you have to get information - for example, if you have to study the market and collect cost data - it can take longer. If your first estimates prove to be wildly out, then revising the plan and re-working the sums will take time.

I am afraid there are a lot of questions to answer, and a lot of sums to do. The arithmetic is not really difficult. If you can add, subtract, multiply and divide, that's about all you need. But you must do the sums. Be careful and methodical. You must get a feel for the figures. You must form your estimates, however difficult it may be.

You must be clear about one thing. A business plan is *not* a blueprint to be followed meticulously through, as if you were making an aeroplane out of a kit. A business plan is a means of mapping out the scene so that you (and others) can make better decisions today in the light of what might happen tomorrow. So you do *not* have to get it right - only as good as you can in the light of the information you have. Better information should make it better, but never perfect. Once you have the plan, use it as the basis of your management systems, updating your estimates and forecasts in the light of actual figures that emerge as you trade.

Business planning is hard work - but fun. Have fun.

Ron Johnson

Guildford
May 1990

Note for the Third Edition

In the second edition the original text was expanded to take account of the appearance of the internet, the needs of organizations that apply for grants from public bodies, and Consultants helping businesses in the newly democratic countries in Eastern Europe.

In the three years since the second edition was published the internet has become a major force in the business world. Anyone who now embarks on the initial production or a revision of a business plan must take the internet into account. The book has been revised and a new chapter on internet planning added to enable you to see where you need to include this in your plan. The new text has been cross-referenced to appropriate sections of the book.

Once again I am indebted to Martin L. Smith, FCA, FILog, FCIT, FInstD (Business Consultant) and Mark L. Johnson, BSc, ACA (Financial Projects Manager, BOC Group) for helpful discussions and for their assistance in the preparation of the new chapter. Any errors or omissions must, however, remain my own responsibility.

The internet is an added complication, but also a stimulating challenge. If you do not weaken, it will add to the fun.

Ron Johnson
Guildford
April 2000

PLANNING TO PLAN

> **OBJECTIVE: to review the process of planning and the elements of a business plan, and on that basis, to prepare a programme of work to complete the business plan.**

- **How to get started**

- **What information you need to assemble**

- **The initial decisions you need to make**

- **The sales and marketing decisions you must face**

- **How to plan your financial strategy**

- **Putting it all together**

- **Making up a planning timetable**

This chapter deals with how to get the planning process started. It will help you draw up a programme of action to prepare your business plan. We shall examine the make-up of a plan and the steps you must take. You must then consider the people involved and the work required, and on this basis, set yourself targets and a timetable. This timetable should be written down and talked through with the people whose support you will need (see Figure 1).

If you have already been trading you may find it easier to answer many of the questions. But it is very important in planning to *look at everything afresh*, to question every assumption and to build up the plan from scratch.

A business plan is typically for three to five years. Since planning involves to some extent trying to predict the future, the longer the plan the more speculative it becomes. But business plans of less than two years are scarcely worth the effort.

Figure 1 Planning Timetable

ACTION	PEOPLE & METHODS	TARGET DATE	DONE BY
1. Plan the plan			
2. Consider the internet			
3. Decide the purpose			
4. Enlist support			
5. Define the business			
6. People profile			
7. Scan the market			
8. Scan the environment			
9. Identify your niche			
10. Pricing policy			
11. Location and address			
12. Forecast sales			
13. Marketing strategy			
14. Forecast expenditure			
15. Capital expenditure			
16. Forecast profit/loss			
17. Turnover and stocks			
18. Forecast cash flow			
19. Review funding			

20. Revise business plan

21. Information systems

22. Complete plan

23. Check viability

24. Implement plan

25. Update the plan

Note All the activities on this checklist must be completed, but since each decision has implications for others, every early decision must be kept under review as the plan develops. In many cases more than one activity can be carried out at the same time.

GETTING STARTED

You will need to spend time deciding who will use the plan and why ('The Purpose of Your Plan' – Chapter 1). Decisions about this will enable you to decide on who will be involved, how much detail you need and how the plan should be put together and presented.

The internet is now a major factor in business. Take a little time to consider the potential applications of the internet on your business and your plan (see Chapter 2). You will need to consider internet usage in more detail at each stage, so now focus only on its potential advantages.

Consider the people who will help you to draw up the plan ('Enlisting Support' – Chapter 3). There are two aspects to this. The people whose support you will need to put the plan into effect (your colleagues and senior managers, and those who will lend money or invest in the venture), and those whose expertise you may need to assemble information and to put the plan together (for example, coping with specialist topics, such as market intelligence, taxation, property, contracts).

To 'Define Your Business' (Chapter 4) can be one of the most difficult problems. It is not good enough to make bland statements about the kind of business you are conducting. This lack of clarity can lead to the dissipation of managerial effort over several different market segments, covering several types of products or services, using a variety of techniques. For small to medium-sized companies, this generally leads to disaster.

Success lies in making a very clear and crisp statement about what the firm aims to sell, and to whom and at what price/quality mix, and by what means, and in following these through with vigour. If the aims are based on a sound analysis of the market and of the firm's strengths and weaknesses, there is a good chance of success.

The definition you produce becomes the starting point for considering the people you need and the market-place you need to scan; but you may need to review this definition of your firm's aims, and perhaps even revise it dramatically, when you have completed the market analysis.

This also has a bearing on the location of your business. In some businesses, the actual location where customers will visit or the address from which you trade will be of crucial importance. The location you choose will also have an important bearing on its cost to your business.

ASSEMBLING DATA

You and the people you gather around you to run the business are crucial to its success ('People Profile' – Chapter 5). You need to take a good hard look at your knowledge and abilities. Together, do you have what it takes to tackle each aspect of your chosen business? If not, what are you going to do about it?

Once you have decided, provisionally at this stage, what business you want to be in, you will need to consider:

• Your potential customers
• Your competitors
• The environment in which you, your customers and your competitors are
  working

('Scanning the Market' – Chapter 6 and 'Scanning the Environment' – Chapter 7.) Experience has shown that an effective way to get to grips with the complexities of the environment is to consider, in turn, the political, economic, technical and social situation.

INITIAL DECISIONS

In the light of the information gathered in your market scan, you may need to review your definition of the business, identifying more precisely the segment of the market you plan to serve ('Identify Your Niche' – Chapter 8). This will enable you to estimate what products and services you propose to sell, what prices you will charge and what methods you will choose to reach your potential customers.

Fixing the prices for your goods and services is no easy matter ('Pricing Policy and Profit' – Chapter 9). Make them too high and nobody will buy them. Make them too low and you will lose money. But there is more to it than that. You need to fix the price and quality according to where you have decided to be in the market-place. You can buy a pen for 20p or £10: Different pens, different parts of the market-place.

Where is your business located in the market-place? Making inexpensive items and selling them in large quantities? Or making a few and charging a great deal of money for them because people value them and are prepared to pay?

Many new companies start by identifying a 'gap' in the market-place, a need that nobody else is meeting, a market 'niche'. But to do this successfully means identifying precisely what to offer, and at what price.

Rarely does it make sense to work out the cost per unit and then add the required profit to fix the price. This may be necessary in some kinds of business, but it is in most cases approaching the business backwards. Having identified the product or service, and the right price, you must work out a way to provide it – and make a profit!

Before you can make any final decisions about pricing policy, you will need to consider the financial information about costs and profitability factors (Chapters 13 to 17).

As part of your planning activity, you may wish to review the legal form of your business: will it be best as a sole tradership, a partnership, a co-operative, a limited company; or are you aiming to trade in its shares? You must have expert advice on such a decision. The key factors include the extent of business risk, the sharing of authority, responsibility and risk, the disclosure of information, freedom of manoeuvre, and financial, especially taxation matters.

You will need to consider afresh where you will site your business in the light of your decisions about the market ('Location and Address' – Chapter 10). You may decide to operate from one site, which may involve design, manufacture, storage, trading, demonstration, distribution, servicing, and so forth. Your business may not involve all of these functions, but as the business grows, it may be wise to consider the location for each function.

As mentioned previously, there are two aspects to the location decision. One aspect is concerned with the image and trading situation, and the other with the costs involved. Availability of suitable employees is another factor.

SALES AND MARKETING DECISIONS

A knowledge of your market-place, the customers, their requirements, your competitors and their particular strengths, coupled with your decisions about what to sell and how, will enable you to estimate what you will sell, and what income will be generated from sales ('Sales Forecasting' – Chapter 11).

If we assume that you have already decided in broad outline what your marketing strategy will be, you will now need to put a lot more flesh on the bones ('Marketing Strategy' – Chapter 12). You will need to specify in more detail how you intend to inform and reach your customers, how you expect them to respond, how you will react to their response, make a sale, provide the goods or services and collect the revenue.

According to the nature of your business, you will need to consider advertising, exhibitions, sales promotions, telephone selling, sales representatives, distribution systems, invoicing and customer record systems, credit facilities, and so forth.

You will also need to consider your 'corporate identity'. In what light do you wish to be seen by your customers and the public? Do you wish to be firmly associated with one kind of business? Do you wish to appear substantial and respectable? Do you want to appear prestigious and exclusive – or inexpensive? This will have an important effect on your company or business name and how you want this represented.

FINANCIAL STRATEGY

Now that you have some idea about how the business will operate you can start to write down in detail the costs involved in running the business ('Expenditure Forecast' – Chapter 13). For the run up to the beginning of trading and for the first year of the plan you will need a month-by-month forecast of what you will spend, and when payments will become due. For the second and subsequent years a quarterly forecast will suffice.

Your business is likely to involve expenditure on capital items, for example, cars, premises and equipment ('Capital Expenditure and Liquidity' – Chapter 14). You will need to identify these capital items separately, to specify when you will need to acquire them, how you will finance them and how long you consider they will perform effectively – before they become unreliable or obsolete. Remember that there may well be advantages in leasing capital equipment.

Armed with a knowledge of what you expect to earn in each year, and what costs can be attributed to the provision of the goods and services concerned, you can calculate the anticipated profit or loss ('Profit Forecast' – Chapter 15).

Beware. This is not a simple calculation. Be careful to ensure that you understand the methods you must use. You may find it useful to calculate the profit and loss on a monthly basis, but *do not confuse* this with the cash flow forecast. These two calculations give you quite different information, and they are used for two different reasons.

Do not be surprised if you find that the business is not making a profit to begin with. This often happens. The key questions are (a) how long will it take to achieve profitability and (b) taken over the first two or three years, will the business be worth running? If you find that the business is not reaching the desired profitability levels, you may need to do some radical re-thinking about your market niche, and the definition of your business.

If you are involved with products or services that require you to hold materials in stock, whether they be finished goods for sale, raw materials, components or spare parts, it is important to consider the quantities you will store ('Turnover and Stocks' – Chapter 16).

The temptation is to keep plenty of materials around you to deal with any situation that may arise. But there are several reasons for looking at this in more detail. Goods in store take up space, and you have to pay rent and rates on that space – money that could otherwise be earning interest. Goods in store might become obsolete or deteriorate and hence lose value.

The level at which you keep stocks must be considered carefully, taking full account of the cost implications, delivery times from suppliers, rate of use and the importance to the business of adequate stocks.

From your forecasts of sales and estimates about when payments will be received, together with your estimates of when bills must be paid, you can draw up a forecast of the cash flowing into and out of the business ('Forecast Cash Flow' – Chapter 17).

This forecast is a vital management tool. It must be prepared on a month-by-month basis for the first year, and quarterly for the second and subsequent years of the plan. On this basis the firm's requirements for cash will be known. Once the basic business plan is clear, you will need to set up systems for monitoring the actual cash flow (Chapter 20) in comparison with what you have predicted, so that you can anticipate and deal with a shortage of ready cash to pay bills.

If you do not update your cash flow predictions, there is a very real danger of running out of money and becoming, in effect, bankrupt and unable to pay bills. It is quite possible to be making adequate profits but become bankrupt in this way, and for the business to fail when it appears to be successful.

In the light of the cash flow forecasts the financial underpinning which the firm requires can be determined, taking into account the anticipated investment by the owners, sources of loans and judicious use of leasing methods ('Funding Review' – Chapter 18).

PUTTING IT TOGETHER

With most of the pieces of the plan gathered, they must now be put together ('Revise Your Plan' – Chapter 19). A typical outline for a business plan is provided in Figure 2. You may wish to vary this outline in the light of your own particular business, but you should consider carefully each of the headings and ensure that the answers to key questions are covered in each case.

Figure 2 Outline of Business Plan

Name of the business

Address of the business

Nature of the business

People in the business

Marketing and sales strategy

Profit and loss forecasts

Cash flow forecasts

Capital expenditure plans

Stock purchasing policy

Funds required – financial base

Book-keeping – management information systems

Special factors and risk assessment

Action plan – key decisions – target dates

Before you put the plan into effect you should consider carefully how you will keep track of your firm's performance ('Management Information' – Chapter 20). How will you monitor sales? How will you keep up to date on receipts and payments, and update your cash flow forecasts? How will you control your stock levels?

In effect you will be building up the plan section by section as you proceed

('Complete Your Plan' – Chapter 21). Now is the time to pull all the sections together and check for internal consistency.

There are no 'sure-fire' ways to predict whether a business will succeed or fail, but there are some pretty useful indicators ('Check for Viability' – Chapter 22). When the chips are down, there are three types of factors to consider: the men and women who will run the business; the market-place and practicality of the business idea; and the management of money.

To put your plan into effect, you will need to work out a simple 'critical path' ('Implement' – Chapter 23). The order in which actions are taken can materially affect the speed with which you can make progress and get your business or your new initiative off the ground.

Almost as soon as the ink is dry on the plan some new factor is likely to arise ('Updating the Plan' – Chapter 24). It might be a change in the cost of fuel or a major component of your product, or the appearance of a new competitor. Refer to your plan and you will soon see whether any major changes are needed.

The very existence of your plan, the information you have assembled and the thought you have given to your business will enable you quickly to take account of the new factor, consider the implications and decide on what action to take.

Apart from these responsive modifications to your plan, you should get into the habit of updating the business plan on an annual basis, rolling it forward one year and firming up the first year on a month-by-month basis in the light of your experience and the current situation.

PLANNING TIMETABLE

As you can see, many of the decisions cannot be taken until quite a bit of the information has been assembled. Thus, in drawing up your timetable for planning, the essential steps are:

- Decide why you want the plan
- Become familiar with what a plan looks like
- Decide who will help you draw up the plan
- Describe the kind of business you want to run
- Gather information about the market and the environment
- Gather information about costs
- Make some forecasts and do your sums
- Revise your business ideas
- Check for viability
- Revise monitoring procedures
- Work out your 'critical path'
- Pull it together and go for it

Part One

GETTING STARTED

Chapter 1

THE PURPOSE OF YOUR PLAN

OBJECTIVE: to decide on why you are writing the plan before you start detailed work. This chapter will help you to make this key decision and to consider how it affects the way you will work.

■ **Be clear about why you are preparing a plan**

■ **Identify those who will make decisions based on your plan**

■ **Itemize the factors which investors and lenders will look for**

■ **Consider the management decisions involved**

■ **List the people who will help you draw up the plan**

■ **Recognize the value of planning and give it some priority**

■ **Compile your own checklist of key factors**

The first step in the planning process is to decide just why you are undertaking the exercise. Business planning is *not* about producing a blueprint to be slavishly followed through, line by line. It is about pulling together all the information you can in a sensible way to *enable people to make better, more informed decisions today*, not to make tomorrow's decisions.

In general, businesspeople prepare business plans:

• When they start out
• When they see a need for a change in direction
• As part of an ongoing review process

This book assumes that you are not simply rolling forward a five-year plan, but that you have decided to take a long, hard, deep look at what you want to do over the next five years, and that you want to plan properly for this.

Careful planning will help you to make better decisions and avoid costly mistakes.

PEOPLE INTERESTED IN YOUR PLAN

Three groups of people make decisions based on your plan:

- The people who will invest in the business, the equity shareholders if you have a limited company
- The people who will lend money to the business
- The people who will run the business on a day-to-day basis

You may be applying for a grant from a public body (for example an agency or department of a Government agency or of the European Commission). In this case the officials of the body concerned will be a further group of people with a keen interest in your business plan.

Those who will give credit terms on supplies are also, in effect, lending money to the business and will need to be satisfied that it is credit-worthy. Such people do not usually study the business plan, but establishing your credit-worthiness with such people must be included as part of your plan.

In Figure 3, list the people who you expect to read the plan and make decisions based on it – including yourself (as investor as well as manager?). If you have senior managers, the list should also include them: they will each have a particular interest according to their specialism, for example, marketing, production, engineering, or whatever.

From time to time, as the planning process proceeds, you will need to check that each of these groups of people will gain what they need from the final document. What will each group of decision-makers look for in the plan?

Investors and lenders

The people who invest in the business or lend it money are looking basically at two factors: first, at whether or not, within a reasonable period, the business will earn more money than it costs to run; second, whether the rate at which cash will flow into the business will enable it to meet each demand for payment as it arrives. In other words, they are looking for profitability and cash flow.

Figure 3 People Interested in the Business Plan

On the left hand side, list all the people who will make decisions based on the plan. Remember that it is the people who make decisions, not companies, banks or public bodies. Be careful to specify in each case the individuals who will play a key part in the decision.

On the right hand side, write down what you consider they would wish to see in the plan: in other words, the basis for their decisions.

DECISION-MAKERS   **DECISION FACTORS**

(Investors)

(Lenders)

(Managers – make a note of
their specialist interest)

(Officials in Grant-awarding bodies)

Investors and lenders will ask a number of 'what if' type questions: for example, they might look to see whether the business has the financial resources to fund any expansion plans, or to weather the effect of higher-than forecasted sales. High sales figures may appear superficially attractive, but they could lead to cash flow problems: for example, when your company is required to pay for more raw materials and equipment to fund production, whilst income from sales is taking longer to arrive.

Alongside these factors they will be making judgements about whether their investments or loans are secure, and taking into account the relative proportions of loan money to investor's money supporting the business and whether or not any of this investment is related to tangible assets such as land, buildings or saleable plant and machinery.

Investors and lenders will look behind the figures at what assumptions have been made about costs, sales, and so forth, and above all at the competence of the people who will be running the business. It is helpful to include a curriculum vitae for each key manager, showing his or her unique contribution to the future business.

Thus the written document must be designed to enable people to make these judgements and this can be used as a kind of yardstick against which to assess the quality of the business plan.

Grant-Awarding Bodies

If you wish to apply for a grant from a public body you must consider the concerns of the officials with whom you will be dealing. It is likely that they will have two overriding concerns:

1. The objectives of the grant. Generally speaking when a public body offers a grant, the scheme forms a part of an overall strategy to bring about a change of some sort. The strategy may be, for example, to improve the prosperity of a geographical area, to encourage a particular type of trade, to generate employment, or to accelerate the introduction of new technology.
2. The viability of the organization to whom the grant is given. It will bring no credit to the officials or the public body if they give a grant only to find that the organization fails to deliver.

It follows that when you are preparing your business plan and engaging in discussions with these officials you must clearly demonstrate how the activities of your organization will help to further the strategic aims of the public body. This factor is over and above the requirements of an ordinary business plan, but essential if you are dealing with a grant-awarding body. Study carefully the aims and objectives of the public body as well as the criteria for the award of a grant. From these studies you will be able to see how to draw up a plan that meets business objectives and also contributes to public policy development. It will also help you in the way you write the plan and present its key features. If, for example, the grant is associated with employment generation you will need to estimate the number of jobs the business will generate and when. Hopefully these will be new jobs, that is not jobs effectively transferred to you from another local employer because you take away his or her business. Public officials tend to judge viability on the quality of the people who will manage the operation as well as the validity of the written plan. It is vital to include a detailed curriculum vitae for each of the key managers who will be involved in running the business when applying for public funds. This section should show the expertise and experience that they will bring to the operation to make it a success. Public officials are also likely to be interested in the extent to which these managers have been forged into a team who are dedicated to the organization's goals.

Managers and planning decisions

Those who will manage the business on a day-to-day basis will need to be assured of its financial viability – the same basic data as that required by investor and lenders. They will also need to know, from the plan, what are the key indicators of performance, which expenditure figures to monitor closely, how to judge sales performance, which targets are crucial to success, and so forth. They will need to know how sensitive the business is to fluctuations in the price of fuel, raw materials, labour costs, and what policy it is sensible to adopt on discounts to customers.

If you and your colleagues who manage the business are closely involved in drawing up the plan, you will find the process valuable in itself in highlighting the key assumptions and factors that influence success or failure. As the situation changes, you will also find that the information you have assembled for the plan and the insights you have gained will improve the quality of your decisions and those of your senior people on a day-to-day basis.

You will not need higher mathematics to deal with the financial side of the plan. The basic work can be done with a pencil and paper, provided you can add, subtract, multiply and divide, although it speeds things up to use a calculator, or better still if you know how to use it, a computer. If you use a calculator, I recommend the use of a printing calculator because it makes it easier to trace arithmetical errors. An accountant will help you to deal with some of the more sophisticated aspects of financial planning.

The manager in charge of each function or activity in the business will learn from the planning process the key parameters of his or her function. The manager will appreciate in particular:

- Where costs arise
- Where and how the activity contributes to business success
- How the function relates to other parts of the business
- What relationship should be developed with other key people in the business
- What areas of the activity need to be monitored closely, what figures need to be collected and compared with the planned performance

Consider Figure 4 overleaf and for each activity seek to establish likely performance measures that should be monitored closely. Some examples are given below, but these serve only to illustrate the point. You must work out the measures which are relevant to your particular business.

Figure 4 Key Decisions and Performance Monitors

ACTIVITY

Advertising

Sales

Manufacture

Distribution

Financial control

Purchasing and stores

Field service engineers

Examples of decision areas and measures of performance

Advertising

• Budget for advertising
• How the money will be spent
• Number of enquiries generated
• Cost per enquiry generated, preferably attributed to each medium as far as this is possible, for example, by coding
• Advertising cost per completed sale
• Number of hits on the web site per day, week, month

Sales

• Methods used for interfacing with customers and closing sales
• Sales mix (where there are different kinds of products/services)
• Number of sales
• Cost of sales department per sale
• Time taken to respond to enquiries
• Number of sales through the internet, per week, per month

Manufacture

- Methods of manufacture to be used
- Cost per item produced
- Labour cost per item produced
- Cost of raw material per item produced
- Levels of work in progress
- Wastage of raw materials
- Other associated costs

Distribution

- Warehouse size/location
- Cost per pack/carton moved
- Cost per vehicle mile
- Picking accuracy
- On time deliveries
- Productivity – cartons per hour work
            – cartons per trip

Financial control

- Terms of trade
- Invoicing, statements, debt collection methods
- Cost per invoice
- Amount of creditors due
- Number of invoices unpaid
- Other associated costs

Purchasing and stores

- Cost per order placed
- Levels of stocks maintained (raw materials, finished goods, spare parts)
- Storage costs

Field service engineers

- Number and geographical distribution
- Cost per service call
- Time taken to respond to request for service
- Customer satisfaction

For each significant activity in the company you will need to set out how it will be done and targets for performance. Where possible, financial figures for budgets and targets should be derived from zero-based budgeting: in other words, building up from basic factors, such as on the anticipated consumption and costs of raw materials, the time taken to perform various functions, the anticipated use of services, the power consumption of key equipment, and so forth.

In any organization, it is all too easy to build in 'fat' over the years, and re-examining these figures from scratch will cause managers to justify each item of expenditure and the use of time. Early attempts at estimating may prove difficult, and you may need the help of experts.

Don't spend time calculating figures very precisely, but work hard to ensure that your estimates are realistic. Spend time on the crucial figures, and use rough estimates where the costs are relatively minor.

COSTS AND BENEFITS FROM PLANNING

The main cost in business planning is undoubtedly the time of directors and senior managers. The difficulty in persuading busy directors and managers from the hurly-burly to spend time in planning is one of the reasons why some firms use management consultants. Quite apart from any expertise they bring, they stimulate managers and help them to gain the collective will and discipline to plan.

The benefits from a properly conducted corporate strategy review and business planning exercise involving the board of directors and key senior managers can be summarized as follows:

- The managing director, other board members and senior managers gain a thorough understanding of the business, its environment, its strengths and weaknesses, its opportunities and threats: in other words, they have a *realistic overview* of the business
- The managing director, other board members and senior managers gain a shared vision of where the company is going, what its goals are and how they will be achieved: in other words, they gain a *sense of direction* and purpose
- The managing director, other board members and senior managers gain an understanding of the key decisions in the business and the part which each department will play in achieving results: in other words, they are well placed to co-operate and *work as a team*
- The managing director, other board members and senior managers will have reviewed each key contact, for example, with their customers,

suppliers and investors, and will know what to look for to help the business prosper: in other words, they will know how best *to deal with customers, suppliers and investors*

- The written plan can form the basis of a system of objective-setting, enabling each section of the company to set goals which demonstrably *contribute to business success*
- Because of their deeper understanding of the business, the managing director, other board members and senior managers will be better placed *to respond quickly, intelligently and effectively* to new situations that arise
- Because of the detailed analysis and data gathering that have been undertaken, the board will be well-placed *to secure the financial backing* required to implement its plans

You will notice that the major gains are for the management team of the company. The written document itself does not provide evidence to investors and lenders, but it does provide a starting point for a penetrating conversation with the board and senior managers of the company. If the management team can explain the plan, defend the data and the conclusions drawn from it, and convince the investors and lenders that the proposals are viable, and that the team of people who will lead the enterprise have the ability to succeed – the plan will have served a valuable purpose.

PEOPLE INVOLVED IN PLANNING

Ideally, everyone involved in the company should be involved in the planning at some level. This is not always possible in practice, but the important thing to remember is that you must consider every facet of the business as the plan is drawn up. In a small business, as each section of the plan is prepared, care will be needed to ensure that the correct research and investigation has been conducted and the appropriate advice has been taken. It is crucial for you to ask the right questions, and general guidance is given in later chapters; specialist advice, however, may be needed in relation to the nature of the business.

If you have some managers or people with specialist knowledge of the business, their advice and views should be sought and, where appropriate, they could join the planning team. There will be some areas where outside specialist advice may be required, in, for example, taxation planning and insurance matters, and in areas such as employment legislation, health and safety matters.

If your firm needs to enter into formal business contracts or agency agreements, legal advice is desirable. Specialist advice will be needed if the firm is

Figure 5 People Involved in Planning

On the left hand side, list the key factors you can identify which will impact on the business plan. As your work proceeds you may find that you must add further factors, so you will need to keep this list updated.

In the second column, list the people who will help you with this aspect of the plan, and in the third column, indicate whether they are to be included in the planning team (put 'T') or to be consulted (put 'C') as required.

A few headings have been included to get you started, but you can cross these out if you find that they do not apply to your business.

FACTOR	PERSON	INVOLVEMENT	Date consultation PLANNED	OCCURRED
Internet applications				
Sales forecast				
Production				
Promotion				
Purchasing				
Delivery				
Sales and invoicing				
Pricing policy				
Tax planning				
VAT				
Employing people				
Health & safety				
Contracts				
Computers				

concerned with patents, trade or service marks.

Thus, apart from board members, there may be people within the firm who should be involved in the planning process, and there are people outside who will need to be consulted. Use Figure 5 to prepare a checklist of the areas which will need to be covered in preparing your plan, and the way you will gain the help and advice you need.

Remember that by involving key people in the planning process, you will help them to gain insights into the reasons for your decisions and to be committed to making it work out in practice. A business plan has many parts that need to fit together and talking it over with other people involved will help you see the plan from several angles.

There may be occasions when you and some members of your management team will need to visit investors, lenders or public officials. On such occasions the people who have been involved in the business planning process are likely to be more convincing – both as team players and as people who are committed to the plan and believe in it. This belief is not based on blind trust, but on working through the detail of how the thing will work.

In my experience managers who have worked together on a business plan (or indeed any kind of plan) are likely to display their familiarity with the plan and faith in its execution in discussion. It is more difficult for people who have not been involved in the plan's creation to demonstrate that they are convinced of its viability.

Chapter 2

INTERNET PLANNING

> **OBJECTIVE: to review the potential applications of the internet in your business and to decide how to integrate these ideas into the business planning process. At this stage do not get bogged down in the detail. You can get into that when you have a clear idea about where the internet will be useful, and where it will not be helpful.**

- **Secure a basic grasp of what the internet is about**

- **Survey the areas where it might help your business**

- **Be aware of some of the pitfalls and precautions required**

- **Review how you will manage information within your organization**

- **Think through how you will deal with external contacts of all kinds**

- **Choose your internet service provider with care**

- **Be selective in the applications you use at the outset**

It is difficult to know where best, in the planning process, to consider your use of the internet. In some ways you will not be able to answer some of the key questions until your business idea has been developed. But being aware of the possible applications of the internet will help you to formulate your business plans in a modern context. Thus, it will be helpful to read this chapter before you work on defining your business, and you will need to return to this subject again once your ideas become clearer.

No business today can ignore the World Wide Web and the opportunities afforded by the internet, e-mail and other digital tools. Your competitors will certainly be using these tools. Your customers and collaborators will expect you to be accessible through this medium. You must spend time at this stage thinking through the possible applications of the internet in your business, and talking it through with your colleagues.

The e-mail has become, for many, the communication method of choice. It is quick and vast amounts of information can be transmitted directly to your contact's computer for immediate use. Articles for publication, copy for advertisements and so forth can be sent online and viewed by your contact on his or her computer screen within minutes, ready for processing.

If you are not yet familiar with the internet you may need to consult a simple introductory text to understand some of the words and phrases used in the following section. It is not enough to know the jargon, you need to have a basic understanding of how the internet works in practical terms.

But beware. Take a balanced approach. It is easy to become seduced by the wonder of the tools and get carried away with your enthusiasm and to waste time and money. It is also possible to get bogged down in the complexity of all the possibilities and the jargon. If you don't know very much about the internet and your business is likely to be a modest one to start with, focus on just two or three applications. I suggest you seriously consider three applications: e-mail, a web site and data acquisition. Most serious business people now communicate by e-mail. If you want to announce your presence to the world, you need a web site. There is an enormous amount of information available quickly and cheaply on-line. Capture that data. When you collect information from the internet, be sure it comes from a reliable source. There is a lot of misinformation and pure rubbish out there. Some of it is free and some will cost you money. Learn how to get at the best, reliable information fast and cost-effectively.

What is the Internet?

The following explanation is not intended to be an authoritative account, but it may be enough to set you thinking. It is no substitute for a proper study of the subject and sound advice. In effect, the internet (the net) is a massive collection of permanently connected computer networks. If you connect to one of these through your computer and a telephone line you become 'on-line' and are potentially connected to all of these computer networks. The normal method of connecting a computer is to the telephone line through a modem, and nowadays this is often included in computers as supplied. You also need some software. Mobile telephones with WAP (Wireless Access Protocol) can also access the internet. In this book the term 'intranet' is used to describe a network of connected computers, typically for an organization, that can be accessed only by the people within that organization.

You can get full internet access by connecting to either an on-line service provider (OSP) like AOL or Compuserve, or an Internet Service Provider (ISP). The OSP or ISP will normally provide the software necessary for you to connect to their system. On-line service providers normally give their customers access to a whole set of information and services carried on a separate network available to people who pay a fee and then connect to the OSP's computer system. The connection to this special net can be independent of the internet, and typically the information there is better organized, regulated and more secure - but obviously limited to what is included. You can, if you wish, operate a small business web site through one of these special OSP nets, with the advantage that people may find it easier to locate your web site (because of the better organization), but access to your web site will, of course, be limited to those who contact that network. Some OSP networks are very large indeed.

Electronic mail (e-mail) is a method of sending messages and text files (with binary file attachments if required) from one computer to another. E-mail addresses are in two parts, typically, a username followed by @ followed by the host name, without any spaces. For example, *Joebloggs@provider.com* would be the kind of e-mail address used by Joe Bloggs if he decided to use an internet service provider called provider.

What computer system will you need? You may need to take advice on this, but key issues to consider include: how fast it will work and how much information it can handle and store, how many terminals you will require and how they will be connected. You will need to consider what ability your system will need to deal with sound and visual effects. Don't scrimp on the screen size. If your people have to work on computers for extended periods, each monitor must be a good size, clear and free from glare.

News groups on the internet provide a forum for people who share an interest to share information. However, as the news groups are usually open for anyone to contribute, some of the information posted may be wrong or misleading. Indeed sometimes it is deliberately so.

SOME BASIC QUESTIONS

The question is not will you use the internet, but how will you use it? Few organizations will be able to ignore the internet for long, and you need to consider what internet strategies you will need to use to become and remain competitive in the 21st century. The internet may, indeed, be the central focus of your business, and not just an optional extra. Check the list in Figure 6 to see where you consider, at this stage in your planning, you are likely to make use of the internet. A description of these areas is given below.

Figure 6 Using the Internet

Most organizations will want to use e-mail, have a web site and surf the web for data!

Potential Application	**Who will prepare a plan?**	**Date for Consideration**
Information Gathering		
Data Capture		
Securing Property		
Internal Communications		
Training		
Digital Forms		
External Communications		
Marketing and Sales		
Purchasing		
Design Collaboration		
Production Management		
Sales Management		
Finance		
Virtual Teamwork		
Busines Adaptation		
Access to Data Warehouse		
Internal Surveys		
Recruitment		

The list is not exhaustive; the internet is changing in its reach and applications daily. But using this list can stimulate your thoughts to consider how you might use it in your own business. Some of the points may arise under more than one heading. That does not matter; you can tidy this up when you have thought through all the possible ways in which you can use the internet to improve your business operation. You may then decide, for each relevant topic, to ask a senior manager to prepare a plan that will provide more details, costs and a timetable for action. You can decide the items you want to include in your plan and the timetable for implementing each part.

Internet technology can bring real advantages to your business, but it also brings with it significant risks. Your planning must include a consideration of these potential risks and how you will deal with them, including the range of computer security issues appropriate to your circumstances. The issues to be considered include, for example, virus protection, routine back-ups, power supply protection, disaster recovery and protection from hackers.

The internet and, if you decide to have one, your intranet, will enable you to gather, organize and disseminate facts and ideas. Using an intranet restricts access to the data to the people who work in your business, and others to whom you choose to allow access. For example you may decide to link your intranet – or parts of it – with that of another organization with which you wish to collaborate very closely. Software is available that can enable you to manipulate the data on the intranet, and to reorganize the data you get from the internet. Web-enabled technology can be used to access databases from the internet and manipulate the data.

Organizations that can trust their employees will wish to make maximum use of the intranet to speed up and manage internal communications. But do remember that 'knowledge is power', and some of the knowledge peculiar to your firm may be dangerous in the wrong hands. The information you decide to hold on the intranet may be commercially sensitive, and its disclosure to a competitor may damage your organization. You must decide the extent to which your employees will be able to send e-mails to people outside the organization.

You must also bear in mind that information is effectively published once it is on the internet (and to an extent on an intranet), and if it is found to be defamatory, you may be liable to legal action. The misuse of the internet by your staff (for example, making racist remarks, or viewing pornographic material) is a matter you cannot afford to overlook. In your plannning, you will need to lay down clear guidelines on its use, and also, I am afraid, monitor that usage. Software is available to enable you to trace every use made by a computer to access specific web sites and to list the destination and so forth of e-mails.

In many ways the intranet and the internet can form a part of your digital toolkit, enabling you to develop your business in new ways. In the future the information that can be handled digitally will enter virtually every aspect of our lives. The combination of the mobile telephone and internet access will open up new applications. Now that computers with enormous power can be minute in size, moving visual images as well as data and sound can be handled digitally. It is worth noting that the data, sound and visual images that can be conveyed over the internet may actually be the product that you are selling to the customer. Data is commonly sold this way and music is sold by being downloaded off the web. Web radio stations that enable you to tune into local programmes anywhere in the world are now well established and web television is heading this way.

INTERNET APPLICATIONS

Information Gathering

There is a lot of information you need to build up a credible business plan - information about your potential markets, suppliers, competitors, relevant legislation and so forth. You will need to decide to what extent this information will be easily sought on the internet.

You can gather information, for example:

- For producing this plan!
- About competitors, their products, services and prices.
- About customers, their needs, wants and buying habits.
- About suppliers and the availability of goods and services you might use.
- On relevant changes in legislation or the rules that govern your business.
- On developments in the science and/or technology that your business employs.

You may find that by periodically scanning relevant news groups and bulletin boards, you will be able to monitor the reputation of your business and products within the net community. Remember, however, that false information can be put on these media.

Data Capture

The ability to access detailed information is a very real advantage of being on the internet, but the way this information is captured and manipulated does need to be thought through and properly planned. You can get software that can lift information from the internet and interchange data readily between databases and spreadsheets.

- Will you have methods for capturing, assessing and disseminating the data you have gathered?

Securing Property

One of the most crucial aspects of the business plan concerns decisions about where you will locate your business and where various functions (office work, storage, production, as appropriate) will be carried out. It is now possible to find out about property availability and costs in various areas on the internet. This is much quicker than trailing around agents, although you will need good advice before making decisions.

- What information about location and property would be useful to your business and how will you get hold of it?

Internal Communications

An intranet can enable people to communicate quickly within your organization. You can also use the intranet to keep people informed about developments in the business. This does, however, mean that people without computer terminals would be at a disadvantage. You could make available your terms and conditions of service and key personnel policies so that managers and staff can quickly check up on any point that is of interest to them – for example about leave entitlement, pension rights or grievance procedures. If your company has important compliance obligations (e.g. financial regulation), the requirements could be posted on the intranet as a reference source. Perhaps the most valuable use will be when people communicate and work together on ideas to improve the business.

- Will you want secure internal communications over a dedicated intranet?
- Will you have an intranet web site to keep your colleagues and employees in touch with developments?
- Will you post your key policy documents, including those connected with employment and human relations, on your intranet?
- Will you seek to manage the knowledge that is central to your organization and its success?

Training

There are considerable advantages to be gained in putting some self-paced learning programmes on a web site on your own intranet. Your employees will be able to learn at their own pace, for example, about your products and services.

- Do you intend to use the intranet as a training tool?

Digital Forms

In the past, people spent a lot of time filling up paperwork forms, ticking boxes and writing down information. Many of these forms could be transferred to the intranet or the internet. If you go down this road, make sure that the output remains digital wherever possible. One of the key issues is how to verify authorizations without a handwritten signature. Organizations have found that most forms can be completed in this way apart from some connected with human resource management.

- Will you transfer much of your paperwork to the intranet or internet?

External Communications

Clearly the major advantage of the internet is the way it enables you to contact people outside the organization quickly. The speed at which detailed data can be transmitted, for example with an e-mail, is often extremely valuable. Remember that material in an e-mail can be regarded as published and therefore any item posted by your staff considered libellous can lead to a legal action against your organization.

- How do you see e-mail being used?
- Who will require e-mail access in your company? How many e-mail addresses will that involve?
- Will you have any rules governing the use of e-mails?

Marketing and Sales

Marketing your organization and its products and services can be achieved through the internet – to those who use it. You will encounter two key problems. The first is to determine how many of your customers will have access to the internet, and be prepared to use it. The second problem is helping people to find your web site amidst the millions out there. Initially you may need to advertise the web site itself, for example by placing advertisements in the kinds of magazines your potential customers read.

If you expect your customers to find your web site through search engines, the wording you use and the search engines with whom you register will be critical: you may need specialist advice. If you want worldwide sales, being in the database of appropriate search engines is crucial. You may want simply to have a presence on the web to alert people of your presence, or to provide information of a general nature that will enhance people's perception of your business.

- Will you set up your own web site?
- What will you expect the web site to achieve?
- Will you design a web site to promote your products and services?
- Will customers be able to purchase from you online? Will your web site enable your customers to interact with your systems or your technical

experts, or your delivery departments to solve problems – for example, connected with delivery schedules or specifications? This will enable you to use personal contact for the more difficult problems and for dealing with more complex, higher value customer needs.

- Will your internet activity replace your normal promotion and sales methods, or be complementary to them?
- How will you ensure that the web site is maintained? The data may quickly become dated and this will annoy those who visit it.

Purchasing

Most suppliers are, or will soon be, on the internet. This means that placing orders for raw materials and supplies can be achieved through this route.

- Will you maintain a watching brief on the sources and costs of supplies through the internet?
- Will you buy supplies on-line?

Design Collaboration

If you intend to design products and services, you may find it helpful to set up secure internet links with your collaborators - inside and outside your organization. Remember that it is now possible to send complicated data and diagrams this way, and to initiate dialogue on design details when the people concerned are thousands of miles apart. You may need careful encryption or a secure link between intranets with your collaborators.

- Will you set up links with design collaborators?
- How will you ensure security for sensitive information?

Production Management

Many organizations have computer systems that help them to manage production and the link with sales and deliveries. This can now be linked to the intranet and it may be helpful to link this with some key business contacts. For example you may want a direct link between your production facility and the company that acts as your distributor.

- Will you use a secure intranet to manage the production of goods and services?
- Will you link this in any way with business collaborators?

Sales Management

Your salespeople will probably use the computer a great deal to manage their portfolios. This information can be gathered together though a unified database. Contact can be maintained through the intranet.

- Will you maintain a classified record of sales on your intranet so that you and your sales people can readily access and analyse the data?

Finance

Computer systems for maintaining accounts have been in use for many years, and many organizations now have systems that enable managers to become intimately involved in the drawing up of budgets and financial plans. The intranet can make this process even more user friendly. You can also conduct your banking business on-line, and seek financial support! There are now advisers on-line that will help you find appropriate start-up funds.

- Will you compile your budgets on-line so that your departmental heads can be involved in setting targets for achievements and monitor income and expenditure?
- Will you train key staff to interpret financial data and become 'business-minded', able to think rationally about productivity, service levels, costs and profitability?
- Do you intend to bank on-line?
- Will you seek financial support through the internet?

Virtual Teamwork

Will you use digital tools to link together your key people into virtual teams across departments and in different locations? This can materially enhance the efficiency of project management across departments and with your collaborators.

Business Adaptation

Will you use the digital information you assemble to guide you in the development and future planning of your business?

Access Data Warehouse

In the past organizations have had different computer management systems for production, sales, invoicing and wages. If you propose to have a system that brings this together in a coherent form within a network, you may wish to access the information from this data warehouse using internet technology.

Internal Surveys

At a later stage you may want to give your employees an opportunity to give you feedback on how they see the company progressing and how they feel about the way they are managed. Instead of using paper and pencil surveys, it is possible to set these up through the intranet, provided every employee can access a computer terminal and knows how to use it. One of the key features of such surveys is the anonymity of replies, and the systems you use must be able to preserve this.

Recruitment

Now that so many jobs are advertised on the internet, it makes sense for you to use it for recruiting – especially if you want people who can use the internet! The range of jobs advertised is very wide, and the medium appeals particularly to professional people. The system allows you to post information about your vacancy and your firm, and also allows applicants to contact you quickly online. You will probably need to work though one of the recognized sites visited by job applicants of the type you seek.

INFORMATION MANAGEMENT

The problem with having access to the internet is that people can waste a lot of time looking for information. You must be very careful in planning and in managing the plan to be highly focused in the information you require, who will get it, from where, and how it will be recorded and passed on to others.

For much of the data handling you will need to establish routines that work well, save time and are user-friendly. You must decide the extent to which everyone who has access to a computer will have access to all the information (apart from highly confidential material such as personnel data). Some organizations allow e-mails to pass freely within the intranet. But do be aware of the fact that if, for example, defamatory remarks about people or organizations are posted on the internet, or even on your intranet, this can give rise to litigation. You will need to establish clear rules for the use of digital tools.

CHOOSING AN ISP

Unless you are intending to provide internet services yourself, you will need to choose at least one Internet Service Provider to give your organization access to the internet, to carry your web site and to deal with your e-mails. In choosing your ISP there are some important points to bear in mind, and many of these are listed in Figure 7. You may be able to add to this list as you consider the needs of your own business. Use the spaces on the right hand side to make notes. You may find it useful to make out a form for each ISP you might use so that you may choose the best one for your business.

The checklist in Figure 7 is suitable for a business where you want occasional access to the internet for e-mail, surfing for information, and maintaining a small web site that provides a few pages of information.

Figure 7 Internet Service Provider

How much will it cost to connect - initially, per month or year, and per second on-line?

How quickly can this initial connection be established?

How reliable is the internet connection?

How quickly is the connection established each time you log on to the internet?

How effective is the support offered? Is it 24 hours every day or only during normal working hours?

Does the ISP offer secure server connection?

How many e-mail addresses will you need? Does the ISP charge per e-mail address?

How much will it cost to prepare and service your web site?

Will you be able to arrange for customers to receive help in connecting to the internet?

What are the arrangements for dealing with search engines?

If, however, you decide to make extensive use of the internet, you will need to consider site hosting, participation in a virtual shopping mall, heavy duty web-enabled applications or continuous internet availability, and more research will be required. If you have a large web site and you expect a large visit rate, you must acquire the ability to handle the large volumes. People quickly get fed up with waiting for your site to load up on their computers.

You may want to offer your customers help in connecting to the internet. The advantage is that you can thereby arrange for your web site to appear every time they connect to the internet. If it is attractive, this may help to promote your business. If it gets in the way of the customers' use of the internet, beware! If you do go down this road make sure that the arrangements you make to provide support are adequate.

In choosing an internet service provider, as well as taking advice and studying the reviews, it is a good idea to try it out yourself at different times of the day and different days of the week - and the support. Most internet service providers offer a free trial period. Some provide merely access and others provide a wide range of information services. You will need to determine what you need and on that basis the most cost-effective service.

BE SELECTIVE

It is easy to be daunted by all these possibilities. Many of them will not be applicable to your business - at least not in the early stages. In each case weigh up the potential advantage to your business against the potential cost, not only in terms of money, but in terms of the management time and energy required to make a beneficial impact. This whole field is moving with extreme rapidity and you must try to keep abreast of those developments that will influence your planning decisions.

Do not be afraid to take a phased approach to the use of the internet. You may decide to focus first on e-mail, a web site and surfing the net for relevant information. The applications that can quickly influence business success such as financial and sales monitoring may follow soon after, whereas setting up training programmes or internal surveys may be considered later. The only caveat is this: if you propose to make any use of the internet, make sure that the computer equipment and software you purchase can be upgraded without too much cost.

Chapter 3

ENLISTING SUPPORT

> **OBJECTIVE: to decide on the expertise and assistance you will need to prepare your plan and to harness these resources effectively.**

- **Assess your own expertise**

- **Bring together your 'planning team'**

- **Start to gather data and write drafts of key sections**

- **Be prepared to modify your ideas as information is gathered**

- **Be prepared to deal carefully with sensitive issues**

- **Consider a 'mission statement' when business aims become clearer**

In the Introduction, you were encouraged to make a start by writing down some first thoughts on the nature of the business, introduced to the component parts of the plan, and encouraged to draw up a programme to prepare your plan.

In Chapter 1, we looked at the people who will need to make decisions based on the plan and through the planning process itself. As you get down to the planning process in earnest, however, you should consider who would actually be involved in the planning process, and what part each person should play. If you are setting up a one-person business then clearly you must write all of the plan yourself, but with help from the many advisory services available.

YOUR EXPERTISE

You must be able to see the business as a whole, to see how the parts fit together and to understand enough about each aspect of the business to ask the right questions and to seek the help of experts where necessary. Be honest with yourself and check out the areas of your knowledge and assess your skills. Use Figure 8 as a starting point.

If you have the time for a course in business planning, you are strongly advised to take one. If you want to set up a very small business, you may find a relevant short course helpful. Try to ensure that the tutors involved are experienced in the management of small businesses, and have the time to provide personal counselling and advice on the programme. You will find that having someone with experience with whom you can talk over your ideas is invaluable.

If you are already in business, attendance at a course may be difficult, in which case you may like to use the help of a management consultant. Do not, however, ask someone else to write the plan for you. The greatest value of a business plan is the understanding that you (and your managers if they are

Figure 8 Your Expertise

Below are some of the areas of knowledge and skills you will need in order to take charge of a business and to draw up a credible plan. The detail may vary according to the business, but this list should provide an initial prompt for your personal 'stock-taking'. Note on the right hand side the state of your knowledge and skills in this area and any steps you intend to take to improve it, if necessary.

TYPICAL KNOWLEDGE AND SKILLS NEEDED FOR SUCCESS

YOUR KNOWLEDGE AND SKILLS

1. The technology of the kind of business you intend to run, the tools of the trade, the methods used, the skills involved.

2. The business parameters of the kind of business you intend to run: for example, typical cost factors, turnover, profit margins, typical contractual arrangements, typical credit terms (buying and selling).

3. Marketing and sales methods: for example, how to research the need for the

products or services, how to estimate demand, how to determine the price and quality, how to identify your market segment, how to reach your customers, the selection of advertising medium, writing advertising copy, technical brochures, selling methods, negotiating with customers, managing a sales force, merchandising methods.

4. Managing money: for example, estimating costs, forecasting and managing cash flow, calculating profit and loss, reading a balance sheet, assessing alternative financial strategies and making decisions about the source and application of funds.

5. Dealing with people: for example, recruiting and selecting the right staff, choosing and working effectively with associates, collaborators, partners or co-directors, managing a team of people, motivating and developing people, gaining the commitment of your staff and colleagues, maintaining effective relationships with customers, suppliers and others crucial to business success – including investors and lenders.

6. You will need to acquire a basic knowledge of the internet and how it can be used.

involved) derive from the thought and work put into it. If someone else writes it, they will get this benefit.

The kind of consultant you want is the one who will take you (and your managers perhaps) through the planning process step by step, so that you learn the key points and can draw up subsequent plans yourself.

You may have sufficient confidence to tackle the exercise without taking a course or hiring a consultant, but be careful to recognize where your knowledge is not good enough, and seek specialist help as required.

At an appropriate stage you will want to talk over your business plan with an accountant and probably with your bank manager, too. It is worthwhile asking other businesspeople in your locality to check out which of the accountants and bank officials are sympathetic towards the smaller enterprise and known to be helpful to people starting out or seeking to impart a fresh impetus to the business. You need enough knowledge to conduct an effective business discussion with these people.

You must recognize that a business plan should cover at least three years, even for the very smallest enterprise. At first sight this seems daunting, as many people find it hard to see even a few months ahead. But a few months is not good enough for business planning. It would be all too easy to set up an enterprise that might survive for a few months, for example, by selling home-made craft items to sympathetic friends and relatives, or setting up a service to meet an evident, but perhaps short-lived demand, only to find that other customers are more distant or more discerning, or that the needs of the identified customers are soon fulfilled or that competitors quickly enter the scene, so that the business fizzles out.

There are other types of business which take time to become established so that the first few months, maybe even the whole of the first year, produce a loss, which must be compensated by adequate profits in the second and third years. If the prospects of profits in subsequent years are not presented in the plan, why would any sane person invest or lend money to the venture?

As a rule of thumb, smaller enterprises should plan to be making a profit by the second year, and this should be clearly indicated in the financial forecasts in the three-year business plan. You must acquire sufficient expertise to draw up a plan which will demonstrate the viability of the business, and which you can present to potential investors or lenders.

THE PLANNING GROUP

If you decide to prepare your plan without involving colleagues, you will need to go through the same steps, but seeking professional help as and when required. Use the checklist in Figure 9 to help you choose when to seek help.

If you are already in business with a small management team, or you intend to start off with some other experienced colleagues, then you should engage in this planning process together. You must discuss each part of the plan between you, although particular sections may be allocated to different members of the team to prepare in draft form.

If you have been running your business for some time and now wish to do some serious planning, you should attempt to draw up a five-year plan,

Figure 9 Specialist Help

Here is a list of some of the areas of expertise and specialists that you may need to call on, and some of the areas they cover which may be important for your business.

Accountant for advice on financial matters, including taxation, social security payments, customs and excise, the effect of different forms of business and financing, dealing with company matters such as annual returns and audited accounts. Do not ignore free advice from the authorities: they will generally answer questions, but not offer suggestions!

Advertising for advice on the best medium to use, and the preparation of copy and illustrations.

Export/Import for advice on markets, sources of supply, documentation and rules. Do not ignore official sources of information and advice: public authorities and your local Chamber of Commerce may be able to help.

Insurance (a) general insurance advice on property, equipment, third party, employer's liability, etc., and (b) specialist on keyman insurances, life insurances and pension matters.

Lawyer help with partnership agreements, property matters and business contracts (but be sure that these are matters the individual specializes in, as there are several different areas of law).

Marketing for advice on methods of gathering and interpreting data about the market-place, customers and their needs. You may get a lot of help from the public library and government survey data, but this needs to be interpreted.

Information Technologist for advice on the use of computers in the business and, if appropriate, access to the Internet and the creation of a Web Site for the operation.

Patent Agent	will generally be able to advise on patents, trade marks, etc.
Property	advice on available property suitable for your business and, in particular, on the conditions of leases, rent reviews, and the like.
Recruitment	advice on the availability of labour, labour costs, cost-effective methods of recruitment for particular kinds of staff you may need. Do not forget the public employment services.
Technical Author	for help in drafting technical literature: for example, manuals and brochures.

although the last few years will be speculative. The discipline of looking five years ahead will require you to look more widely at the changes taking place around you, and will also enable you to take a longer term view of any major changes or investments you might decide upon: for example, major investments in plant, a relocation to a new geographical area or expansion into new markets.

When companies outgrow their premises or the capacity of their equipment, or find that they must update their methods and approaches to stay in the market, then longer term business planning becomes a necessity and not a luxury. The same is true if the market for the business is changing and competitors pose a very real threat.

Thus in a medium-sized firm, you will need to involve in the planning process all the senior people who you want to be committed to putting the plan into action. We will call this the 'Planning Group'. You may need to call on the advice of other experts in the company as well, if they have specific knowledge, insights or judgements to contribute.

You may need some specific help from outside the firm, for example, from a management or business planning consultant, accountant, marketing specialist, insurance broker or on the technical side of your business. Sound advice is rarely free, although there may be subsidized advisory services or consultancy services available.

Once you start to pay for this help, you will need to be very specific in the questions you ask and the results you expect from this involvement. You have the right to expect an initial discussion (for say an hour) free of charge, and you should use this to see whether you can have confidence in the ability of the adviser and whether you consider that he or she will relate well to you, to your Planning Group and to your business. A professional consultant will want to discuss your needs and relate these to his or her own expertise before discussing fees. But following this a reputable consultant will not object to discussing fee rates and what you will get for your money.

Planning group meetings

The first meeting of the Planning Group should consider:

- Why the business plan is being drawn up
- The structure of a business plan
- What they see as the future of the business (what they consider it should be making, selling or providing, and to whom, and how)
- What information is needed to draw up the business plan
- How this information will be obtained and who will get it
- When to meet next to consider progress and to move the planning programme forward

The information you will need includes data about the *environment* of the business, especially the characteristics of potential *customers* and their numbers, the types of products and services the potential customers need (maybe the state of the technology in their sector of industry, for example, in terms of machinery, methods and materials used), the activities of *competitors* or potential competitors, at home and from abroad, the availability of skilled *labour*, the key costs, for example, of buildings and equipment, raw materials, *sources* of supply. If your business is up and running, you will need to pull together key facts – your existing customer base, pattern of sales to your customers, key costs and ratios, potential areas for development, and so forth.

Experience indicates that the Planning Group should meet often, with intervals no longer than three to four weeks between meetings. Any slower progress will result in waning enthusiasm, and information collected for early meetings will be out of date at later meetings.

Aim to complete the planning process within, say, two to four months. This should be achievable even in businesses that are up and running with all the senior people busily engaged in day-to-day management activity. An existing management group will have a sound basis of knowledge and understanding to build on in the planning process – but they must be prepared to open their minds to new situations and new possibilities, and where appropriate, to go back to basics and prepare and justify zero-based budgets.

A Planning Group brought together to plan a new business may well have a good deal of investigative work to do: if this is done properly it will take time, but it is vital if the plan is to be of real value to the business, not only in the pre-start period, but when the business has to be steered through its initial stages.

In the vital matter of identifying potential customers and their needs, you cannot rely on impressions, uninformed opinions and anecdotes. This would mean building a plan on shifting sands. You must, somehow, get out there and find out what people want.

As information is brought together, you may well find that you must refine your ideas about who will be your key customers in the future, just what you will be providing, the best way to reach them, the best way to provide the goods and services, the best location for your business, and so forth.

Sensitive issues

As these ideas develop, you may well find that some controversial suggestions arise that could easily unsettle some of your key staff. You may find it necessary to keep some of these suggestions confidential within the group at the early stages. There is no point in upsetting staff over something that may never happen.

However, if such a suggestion becomes a real possibility, you will need to think through how you will deal with the people concerned as a responsible employer, and then inform them of the possibilities you are considering, how it will change their situations and what provision you intend to make.

As an example, suppose that you consider moving your manufacturing plant from Sussex to Cumbria. Will you want to take some key staff with you? Will they be prepared to go? What help will you give them? What about the people you do not wish to take? Do you want them to work with you up to the last minute? What compensation will you offer them? What help will you give those that are left behind in finding new employment?

These factors must form a part of your plan, but there is also the important issue of how and when information about your plan is communicated to individuals. You should seek to speak to them before these ideas leak out through the local grapevine where people will get a garbled version of what will happen, making them feel insecure, uninformed and unhappy with the management.

Mission statement

It has become fashionable in recent years for companies to draw up a statement encapsulating what they are about: in other words, what their business aims are, who their customers are, what their products and services are, and what distinguishes their business in terms of cost, quality, reliability, value for money or whatever.

At an appropriate stage the Planning Group should set about producing this, but only when they have developed and explored their ideas about what is possible in the market-place and coupled these with the strengths of the business and where they feel they will gain satisfaction and be able to do a job well.

Chapter 4

DEFINE YOUR BUSINESS

OBJECTIVE: to examine critically the business idea and to check this against your initial perception of the market-place so that you may write a first draft 'nature of the business' statement on which market investigations and calculations can be based.

- **Sketch out the key features of your business**

- **Question the nature of your business**

- **Do a 'quick check' on the feasibility of your business idea**

- **Write your first draft of the 'nature of the business'**

Refer to the 'Outline Business Plan' (Figure 2 in the Introduction). It is important to recognize that you do not write such a plan by starting at the beginning. In your final document the name of the business will appear on the front page, but it will probably be one of the very *last* things you decide. The plan will, of course, give the address from which the business will operate initially, if this is known.

The first step is to write down in simple terms what the business is about, what products and services it intends to provide, who will be its customers, and so on. This part may seem easy, but in a new business, people tend to be far too woolly in thinking about this, and existing businesses tend to assume, without thinking, that the customers they have now and the goods and services they provide should be the pattern for the future.

These assumptions have to be challenged throughout the planning process. They cannot be challenged if they have not been articulated clearly in the first place.

QUESTION THE NATURE OF THE BUSINESS

You will will need to produce a rough draft of the nature of the business, but as the planning process proceeds you may well find that this needs to be modified.

Make a start by referring to Figure 10 and write down what it is that you intend to sell, to whom you intend to sell it and what methods you will use. Discussion of a few examples of different types of business may help you to think along the right lines. It is not possible to cover every type of business, but if you grasp the basic ideas from these examples you should be able to work out how to describe your own business.

Figure 10 Key Features of the Business

Below are listed some of the questions you will need to consider as you refine your ideas on the nature of your business. Make a note of your answers to relevant questions and draw these answers together into a succinct statement.

What do you intend to sell?
• Products? How many different types, ranges?
• Services? How would you define these?

Where will be your 'position' in the market?
• High quality and price?
• High volume, low price?

Who will be your customers?
• Individual members of the public? What social class, geographical area, particular interests?
• Manufacturing companies? What size, nature, area? Which managers will make or influence crucially the decision to buy?
• Shops or chains of shops? What kind of shops? What locations (high street, out of town, clustered)?

How will you reach your customers?
• Passing trade?
• Press advertisements? Direct mail?
• Representatives in your employ?
• Advertising on radio or television?
• Advertising on a web site on the internet?

How will you obtain products?
- Manufacture from raw materials?
- Assemble from intermediates?
- Purchase from manufacturer?

How will you provide services?
- Yourself? Plus partners or fellow directors?
- Employees?
- Sub-contractors or franchisees?
- Is your business selling information, for example through the Internet? You may need to advertise a web site through other media if you wish to reach customers.

How will you sell?
- Direct to the public? To manufacturers?
- Through your shop(s)? To shops, individually or by chain?
- By mail order?
- Through a distributor?
- Through the internet or via cable television?
- Telephone sales?

How will you support your sales?
- What delivery will you provide?
- What geographical area?
- What after-sales service?
- What trade terms? What financial help, for example, leasing or loans?

The examples are drawn from manufacture, distribution and sales, and from the service industries, and as you read, look for similar problems and how you will overcome them.

Manufacturing examples

Suppose you want to manufacture articles, for example. Your first thoughts may be: 'The business will comprise the manufacture of metal ashtrays for sale to the general public'; 'The business will be concerned with the manufacture of hand-carved wooden objects for tourists'; or 'The business will consist of the manufacture of high pressure pumps for engineering companies'. But these statements will not do. They leave too many questions unanswered.

How do you intend to manufacture the ashtrays? Where do you intend to manufacture them? How do you intend to sell them? By mail order? If so, you need to state that. (I would not recommend that option in this case!)

Do you intend to sell them to shops, for sale to the public? What kind of shops? Where? Why should these shops buy them?

If you intend to manufacture on a small scale at first, you may well start by selling such articles in shops near to your place of manufacture – if you have reason to believe that you can sell enough to make a profit. As you grow, you may find it better to have a distributor or a sales agent. If you decide to export, particular care will be needed in the choice of people and firms to do business with, and this will involve research.

Thus, although the ultimate customers may be members of the general public, the nature of your business may mean that you are making articles for sale to the general public through distributors or agents, through certain kinds of shops, in certain geographical areas.

Clearly, if you are manufacturing for the tourist trade, you must again decide the way in which you will distribute and sell your goods and the geographical areas where you will work.

Consider the sale of high pressure pumps for engineering companies. Once more you must specify the type of company: for example, size, type of engineering operation, geographical situation, and so forth. In this case, geography is an issue because of the need to transport goods and possibly to provide back-up services, such as maintenance and spare parts.

How will you sell these pumps? Will you sell them by mail order, through distributors, through a network of specially trained salespeople or through engineering craftspeople trained to act as sales representatives, installers and maintenance engineers?

How will you reach key people in such companies? Which people in the companies do you expect to make the purchasing decision? In what way will your particular product appeal to them? How will you present its special properties? Will there be only one pump, or a range of pumps of different sizes and applications?

Distribution and sales examples

Your initial sentences might read: 'The business will consist of a craft shop selling hand-crafted articles and also the materials, tools and equipment used by craftspeople'; or 'The business will involve operating a warehouse where groceries and related goods will be collected together and distributed to grocery shops in the locality'; or 'The business consists of the sale by mail order of a range of household goods'.

The statement about the craft shop business should mention the site of the shop (for example, high street of a well-known and busy town, or in a shopping precinct, or on the sea front of a popular resort), and will hopefully indicate whether you intend to build up a number of regular repeat customers or rely mainly on passing trade.

Will the warehouse distribute to independent grocery shops or a chain? (If a chain is involved, what makes you think the stores will buy from your warehouse? Or do you anticipate having a contract with the chain?)

If you are intending to sell household goods by mail order, what socio-economic groups do you intend to sell to and how will you build up your mailing list? Will you buy lists or advertise in particular magazines? Will you seek to sell your products through the internet? What will these alternatives cost?

Service sector examples

This is often the most difficult area of all to define. Many people have a skill or service to offer, but find it a hard discipline to look at this expertise from the customer's point of view. But a successful business is concerned first and foremost with meeting a customer's need.

Thus, identifying precisely who the likely customers are and what you can provide to meet their needs must be done before you start the business in earnest.

For example you might start by writing: 'The business will consist of the provision of typing services'; or 'The business will be contract cleaning'; or 'The business will consist of hiring out and servicing building equipment'; or 'The business will consist of the provision of consultancy services concerned with garden design and maintenance'. If the internet is to be your main sales avenue you might write 'The business will consist of offering xyz services through the internet.'

But the question is, Who will buy your typing services? Householders (unlikely), large companies (who probably have their own staff, or will hire in temps, rather than contract out typing) or small businesspeople who need occasional typing services? But is that all the office services support they will need? How will the business be operated? Will clients bring their work to you – or will you take it to them?

Who will pay for your contract cleaning? Occupiers of small houses? Large houses? Shops? Offices? Factories? Warehouses? Hospitals? Local authorities? How will you reach the category of customer you seek to serve? If you are proposing to deal with companies or public bodies (for example, hospitals, local authorities), how will you reach the decision-makers and how will you persuade them to award you the contract? In other words, what are the attractive features of your service?

What kind of premises will you cover? How high will you go – the first floor or 20 storeys up? What equipment will you use? How will you ensure quality? How will you recruit, train and monitor your staff? How far will you go, geographically, to get the contract?

If you are in the equipment hire business, will you hire your gear out for long periods (years or months) or for short periods (days or weeks)? Are your customers small builders, middle-sized builders or large companies? How large a range of equipment will you hold in stock? Will you deliver and collect the equipment? Over what geographical areas? Will you own, lease or hire as required the heavy goods vehicles you will need to transport the equipment?

If you propose to offer consultancy services in garden design and maintenance, what size of garden or estate will you deal with? How will your customers come to know of your existence? What will convince them that you know enough about design, plants, the construction of garden features, and so forth? How will you establish your fee rates?

If you intend to concentrate on selling a service through the internet, how do you propose to advertise? Will you need to advertise in a magazine to get people to look at your web site, or will you rely on people finding out about your service through search engines? To get results via search engines you will probably need specialist advice, for example on keywords, and the ones where you will register. You might be able to link with an existing supplier or an online shopping mall. (See chapter 2.)

QUICK CHECK ON FEASIBILITY

Whatever your business, you need to start off with a draft statement of precisely what you are selling and to whom. It is often helpful to state in this section of your plan how you propose to reach your customers and maintain contact with them, too.

It is important to remember, however, that as we move on to the other stages of planning, especially the marketing and financial sections, this original draft may need to be changed as your ideas are subject to financial analysis.

At the outset, check your statement about the nature of the business against the questions listed in Figure 11. Repeat this process from time to time as your planning proceeds. Ultimately every business involves risk. The idea is not to eliminate risk, but to reduce it to an acceptable level. Generally speaking, without risk there is not much chance of real profit.

You *must* be honest with yourself. If there is a weakness in your business idea, you must work through this, modify it if necessary and satisfy yourself and your business colleagues that the risks are acceptable.

Figure 11 Quick Check on Feasibility

Success in business depends crucially on three things:

• Management
• Marketing
• Money

Work through these checklists from time to time as you plan, until you are satisfied.

MANAGEMENT

► Do you and your management team have the motivation and the technical skills to make the products or services you envisage?
► Do you and your management team have all the skills needed to look after the administrative side of the business, including all the money matters?
► Has your organization the ability to sell your goods or services to the potential customers you have identified?
► Are you prepared to modify your business plans in the light of what people will want to buy?
► Are you confident that you and your key managers will be able to manage skills and time to full effect?
► Do you have access to the information technology skills you need?
► Have you and your management team developed the approach needed to deal with the officials of public funding bodies – if that is required?
► Does your management team have the ability to cope with the multitude of demands for compliance with the law, for example in terms of taxation, employment, contracts and environmental issues?

MARKETING

► What is so special about the products that you intend to sell or the services that you intend to provide?
► How do you know that anyone will want to buy them?
► How much will you charge for your products or services? Will people be prepared to pay those prices?
► Are you sure that you can provide those goods or services at these prices, make a profit and manage cash flow?
► Why should anyone buy your goods or services rather than others on the market? Is this the right time to start providing the goods or services that you have in mind? Is this the moment when people will want them?

> ▶
>> Will you be able to develop your products or develop new products as your market develops?
> ▶ Have you considered how you will advertise or promote your products and how much this will cost?
> ▶ Do you know who your competitors are and what products they are selling?
> ▶ Have you spoken to any potential customers about the products or services that you intend to provide?
>
> **MONEY**
>
> ▶ Will your business make a profit?
> ▶ Will you be able to pay each bill when it arrives?
> ▶ What financial resources will you need to be successful, especially over the initial trading period?
> ▶ Are you fully prepared to make your share of this financial commitment?
> ▶ Do you need – can you obtain – a loan at a reasonable rate of interest?
> ▶ Are you confident that you can pay back any loans over a reasonable period, and pay the interest?
> ▶ Have you researched, listed and costed the expenditures that you will incur, and when income will start to flow?
> ▶ Have you analysed the risks – for example of low sales, late payments, scarce raw materials, currency fluctuations – and how you will cope?
> ▶ Have you considered your insurance needs and any licences and permits that will be required?
> ▶ What sources of information, help and advice do you need? Do you know where these can be obtained?
> ▶ Have you discovered any problems that you have never had to deal with before?
> ▶ Have you developed financial management systems that will satisfy public funding bodies – if that is required?

Part Two

ASSEMBLING DATA

Chapter 5

PEOPLE PROFILE

> **OBJECTIVE: to review the skills and knowledge needed to run the business, to plan to succeed through ensuring that the business has these available and to encapsulate this information in a 'people statement'.**

- Recognize the importance of people in your plan

- Itemize the key tasks and areas for decision

- Identify the people concerned and the skills needed

- Decide what option to take to meet the need in each case

- Summarize your decisions in a 'people statement'

THE PEOPLE YOU NEED TO SUCCEED

Having identified the core of your business, you must now decide what skills you and your key people will need to make the business a success.

Use Figure 12 to identify these needs. In some cases you or one of your senior people will possess these skills. In the areas where you are weak, it may be worthwhile updating your skills.

Since the success of your business depends on the skills of the people in charge, this step is vital. People who invest in your business or lend you money will want to know how you intend to cope, and the only way you can convince people is to spell out the key tasks and decisions and state why you think the people you have, or will have, can together deliver the goods.

Figure 12 Skills for Success

First list the skills required (column 1), then the people who should have the skills (column 2). Under the 'action' heading, place a tick if the people concerned have the skills. Otherwise indicate how these skills will be made available to the firm.

SKILLS REQUIRED	PEOPLE INVOLVED	ACTION
Technical skills		
Marketing skills		
Selling skills		
Negotiating skills		
Planning skills		
Costing skills		
Money management		
Quality assurance		
Transport and distribution		
Health and safety		
Information systems		

ITEMIZE YOUR NEEDS

The following checklist should be used in conjunction with Figure 12 to start you thinking about each aspect of the business. There are many tasks to be performed and you need to list the ones which are crucial to your success, and identify the people who will make the key decisions and who will perform these tasks.

Technical skills

- What knowledge and skills do you need in connection with your particular trade?
- What machinery will you use and who will run it and maintain it?
- What procedures and documentation will be used?
- Who will ensure that your firm complies with all the laws and regulations relevant to your trade?

Marketing skills

- What do you need to know about the market-place, the sources of information?
- Who will interpret the data about your potential customers, your competitors and the shifts in demand?
- Who will identify your potential customers?
- Who will ensure that your products and services match the needs of the market-place?
- Who will set the sales targets?

Selling skills

- What methods will you use to reach people and to close the sale?
- What will you need to know about advertising, mailshots, mailing lists, etc?
- To what extent will you need to use cold calls or telesales methods?
- Who will converse with your customers, demonstrate products, describe services, establish customers' needs and desires, deal with objections and close the sales?
- Who will ensure that your sales and marketing efforts are matched by prompt delivery and adequate after-sales service?
- Who can affect the way your firm appears to the potential customer (the 'image' of the firm)? Who will train them and monitor their performance?

Negotiating skills

- What skills and abilities will you need in presenting your case and negotiating with customers, suppliers, backers and officials of public bodies?

Planning skills

- What knowledge and skills will you need in forecasting, costing, budgeting, route planning, critical path analysis?

Costing skills

- What do you need to know about costing your anticipated expenses, costing your overheads, costing your products and services?

Money management

- How will you manage money, monitor your cash flow and profitability, control expenditure, ensure payment for goods and services provided?

Quality assurance

- How will you monitor quality? Who will do it?
- Will you seek official recognition for your quality assurance methods?
- How will you train your people to maintain quality?

Storage, transport and distribution

- Who will manage the storage of goods?
- Are you aware of any special conditions required or particular precautions to be taken in your industry?
- How will you ensure proper stock rotation?
- Will you need a licence to manage heavy goods vehicles? Who is qualified to do this?
- How will you optimize your vehicle routing?
- How will you manage distribution costs?

Health and safety

- How will you ensure compliance with the demands of the law and take all reasonable precautions?
- Will you need a first-aider?

Information management

- How will you set up your management information systems?
- Who will maintain these systems and alert management when necessary?
- What do you know about information storage and retrieval?
- Will you need computer systems? Databases? Spreadsheets? Financial management software?
- How will you choose your systems? Who will use them? Who will interpret the data generated?
- Will you need to access the internet for information? Will you want to use the internet for advertising, for selling or to provide a service? See Chapter 2.

CONSIDER YOUR OPTIONS

Where none of your key staff have these skills you have a number of alternatives: for example, you can plan to recruit someone, or to train someone, or to buy in the expertise as you need it. Indicate in the final column of Figure 12 how you intend to achieve this.

If you intend to recruit someone, you will need to work up a job specification to see how the time of this individual will be spent and the contribution he or she will make to the business. Then you will need a person specification for recruitment purposes. You will need to research the market to find how much you will need to pay, how long it might take to find the right person and what the recruitment costs will be.

If you opt to develop your own skills or one of your colleague's, think through how this will be achieved and what it will cost.

If you decide to use external expertise from time to time, it is worthwhile to identify the people you would use, and to estimate how much of their time you will employ, what it will cost, and when you will use them – for your expenditure forecast.

YOUR PEOPLE STATEMENT

Just as you encapsulated the essence of your business idea in a statement, so you must now pull the important points from this analysis into a statement explaining, in relation to the nature of your business:

- What areas of knowledge and skill are crucial to its success
- What you and your management team have to offer against this
- How you intend to cope with any shortfall

Some backers may want more details about yourself and other key people in your organization. In such cases you may need to draw up and present a curriculum vitae for each key person. This should focus on the individual's qualifications and experience, and indicate how these relate to the needs of the business.

Chapter 6

SCANNING THE MARKET

> **OBJECTIVE: to review the market for your goods and services, the competition you face, and the decisions you need to take to ensure success.**

- Use market segmentation to identify your potential customers

- Assess the impact of your competitors

- Use market survey methods to characterize your potential customers and their needs

In your draft statement on the nature of the business, you described your customers and the goods and services you will provide. Your next step is to study your potential customers thoroughly using every method at your disposal.

Information may be available in written form, for example reference books on specific types of companies, published household expenditure surveys or marketing company reports. Lists of potential customers can be purchased. Useful information about customers may also be available through the internet. There are now books that list web sites of interest to business people.

Finally, you can go and talk to people. If your potential customers are too numerous to tackle in this way you may need to commission a market survey. You need to consider very carefully what information you need and how much it will cost. In many cases you can't beat the 'feel' of talking to potential customers yourself.

SEGMENT THE MARKET

The ultimate aim is to specify your customers as accurately as possible, as this is the information your advertising and sales activities will be based on. There

Figure 13 Market Segmentation

1. List the geographical areas in which you will trade with customers.

Indicate briefly how you intend to service these areas if they are widespread.

2. List the characteristics of the people most likely to buy your goods or services (if you sell to the public).

Indicate any special seasons or purchasing times and places where purchases are more likely to occur.

3. List the characteristics and likely requirements of the intermediaries you hope to do business with.

Indicate the particular types of inter-mediaries who would favour your products and services.

4. List the characteristics of the kind of organizations you want to do business with.

Within these organizations, identify the people (by job title) that you will need to convince of the value of your goods and services to gain sales.

are millions of people and companies in the world and it is folly for a modest-size company to try to sell to everybody. There are a number of ways of narrowing down the list of your potential customers. Refer to Figure 13 as you work through this section.

You can narrow the list down by geography. Do you intend to offer your goods and services worldwide, or just in Europe, or just in England, or just in Yorkshire, or just in Harrogate? If the worldwide market is represented as a circle, segments of the circle can represent sections of the market. Thus we call this process of identifying groups of customers 'market segmentation'.

List the geographical areas where you intend to start trading. You can base your planned marketing and sales activity on these areas, and calculate costs accordingly. There is nothing to stop you from moving into other areas as the opportunity arises – but you will probably incur extra costs and will need to change your financial calculations.

But you can segment the market in other ways. For example, if you are selling to the public, are your products and services of universal appeal or are they likely to be particularly attractive to:

- Young people, middle-aged people, older people?
- Men, women, young men, young women?
- Mums, dads, uncles, aunts, children (for example, Mothers' Day)?
- Fit people, people with a medical complaint or disability?
- Rich people, poor people?
- People with a particular sporting interest?
- People with a particular cultural interest?
- People who want to learn a subject, skill or trade?
- People who work in a particular type of business?
- People keen on DIY activities?
- People keen on travel?

The list is endless, and many of these items combine to narrow down the kind of person to whom you are most likely to sell.

When and where are these people most likely to want to buy your products? When they see a need? When they are gearing up for a sports season or preparing for a holiday? When they are on holiday? At particular seasons or religious festivals? Will they go to a shop in the high street, or to a specialist shop, or buy it by mail through a magazine? Will they surf the internet?

If you sell through intermediaries like chain stores, agents or wholesalers, are there particular requirements they might want? What types of intermediaries will most likely be happy to deal with your products? Will you deal with supermarkets, grocery chains, department stores? Do they prefer particular sizes, shapes, types of packaging, delivery schedules?

If you sell your products or services to manufacturers, commercial firms, public bodies, and so forth, what sizes of organization do you have in mind? Are you interested in the large international bodies and international companies, or government departments, large local authorities and national companies, or smaller firms and smaller local authorities? What do you know about their purchasing procedures and requirements? How will you decide which organizations are most likely to buy your wares?

If you are looking at large organizations, are there particular sections or activities with which you are concerned? Do you want to provide raw materials for the manufacturing section, the garden and parks section, the hygiene and cleansing department, the engineering maintenance department or the training department?

Can you identify in each case the key decision-makers when it comes to purchasing your kind of products and services? In large organizations it is often necessary to convince two or three different people that what you have to offer is worth considering. The purchasing department will have its own priorities, as well as the section that will actually use your materials.

If you are selling capital items, or a part of a contract to a main contractor (for example, in a building project), then you will frequently be helping somebody else to make out a case, and you will have to appreciate not only what your client wants, but what help he or she needs in making out a case that includes your part of the action.

These questions are fundamental to the identification of your particular set of prospective clients or customers – the market segment in which you will operate. Your choice will depend on relating your goods and services, and the particular strengths of your business, to the particular requirements of customers in each segment.

CHARACTERIZE THE CUSTOMERS

At the outset you may have identified a range of goods and services to offer and many groups of potential customers. It is unwise to attempt too wide a range of goods or services, or too many different kinds of customers. Each variation adds to the burden on management. A modest range targeted at a well-defined group of customers is a better way to start.

We have discussed above how to identify the particular group of customers most likely to be responsive to your approach. Now you need to use a variety of means to answer the following key questions. Within the chosen segment you will need to determine:

- How many potential customers you have
- Where they are to be found
- Exactly what they are likely to buy (in terms of quality, size, colour, packaging, delivery, financial terms)
- How much they will buy (quantity to be purchased and frequency)

A detailed discussion of methods for studying the market is beyond this text, but somehow you need to get a 'feel' for your customers. There may be a wealth of information about your potential customers from household expenditure surveys, sector reports on industry and commerce, trade directories, and so forth. Much of this can be accessed through the larger public libraries. Some of this data (for example, about the people who live in different neighbourhoods) may well be on computer files which you can buy into.

Wherever possible, the best way is to go and talk to potential customers about their needs and concerns. The key questions you need to ask in such interviews include:

(a) What kind of business are you in?
(b) What need do you have (for the kind of goods and services concerned)?
(c) How is this need currently being met?
(d) How does this contribute to your business success?
(e) What characteristics do you like about the goods and services you are getting now?
(f) In what ways do you consider that these products and services could be improved?
(g) How are your activities likely to develop in this area over the next year or so?
(h) How do you consider this will alter your demands for the goods or services?
(i) What kind of prices would you be prepared to pay for improved goods and services that met your needs more closely?

Naturally, you must be subtle in the way you ask these kinds of questions, and the phrasing will vary with the kind of products and services you are discussing.

If you are hoping to provide goods and/or services which are quite novel, potential customers may not be able to relate to these until you have demonstrated or explained them. But do not launch into any explanations or demonstrations until you have established answers to questions (a) to (i).

You will also need to make an estimate of the market share you expect to attain – and explain how and why. Remember that if your market share is modest, your competitors may not be too concerned; but as this share grows, you can expect an aggressive response.

EVALUATE THE COMPETITION

Now that you have a clear idea of your potential customers and their needs as they relate to your proposed business, you need to identify the companies that are currently meeting these needs.

Study the size of their operations, the nature and quality of their products, the characteristics of the service they offer, before, during and after the sale. Study the image they present, and see if you can infer, from their advertising, what they consider their advantage to be in the market-place.

Is their strength in dependability? Do they build good rugged machines that go on and on, year in year out, without giving trouble? Do they have a range of goods that just slot into their customers' requirements? Are they up-to-the-minute in sensing their customers' needs and responding; or does it take them quite a while to change in response to a changing market need?

It is by studying factors like these that you will be able to see where you can be different, but in a way that will please prospective customers. There is little point in trying to compete with an established competitor in features where he is strong. You may need to match these – or deliberately take a different line. For example, if your competitor's reliability is dependent on heavily constructed machinery that is difficult to move about, you may decide to make a machine that uses modern materials and design to give strength without excessive weight, and make a virtue out of the portability of the equipment – if your customers will see that as a benefit.

Chapter 7

SCANNING THE ENVIRONMENT

> **OBJECTIVE: to review the environment in which your business is operating as the basis for strategic decisions.**

- Look for the trends in the environment that can affect your business

- Make full use of your managerial talent in identifying the issues

- Examine the political, economic, social and technical issues

- Evaluate the impact and take this into account in your plan

IDENTIFYING THE TRENDS

In any business you need to look at the environment – the current situation and current developments – and to assess the likely impact of impending changes on your business. Foretelling the future is always a doubtful activity. The best we can do is to look around at trends and new ideas and try to estimate which ones are likely to continue, and what impact these are likely to have on each aspect of the business.

Although one is tempted to consider one's own town and country, it is nowadays vital to consider the European scene and, indeed, in some industries the world scene. This is often not as difficult as it seems because if you know your business, you should be able to focus your attention on those aspects which are likely to affect you.

In respect of each development you identify, you will need to consider:

- Whether it will last
- Whether it will grow, decline or change suddenly
- What effect it will have on your industry and on your business

Your business may be affected because the change influences:

- The people who work for you or those you seek to recruit, their aspirations, their expectations, their skills and knowledge: for example, through changes in family structures, housing costs, educational provisions
- The organizations or people you serve, through shifting fashions, changing priorities (for example, a reduction in international tensions, shifts in the spending power of different groups of customers), and hence, the nature of the goods and services you provide
- The way you manufacture, distribute or provide your services as technology transforms working methods and relative costs (for example, between fuel, capital investment, labour) change
- The way you structure your workforce and the pattern of communications: for example, as technology impacts on internal communications and decision-making.

AREAS OF CHANGE

Use this prompt list to stimulate your thinking about the areas which are relevant in your business and complete Figure 14 for yourself. It is not possible to cover every eventuality, but the list should help you to do your own analysis.

Political pressures

- What is the current government posture towards business? Is it on being competitive, getting results, cutting costs, removing barriers to innovation and growth?
- What will be the impact of health and safety legislation, environmental protection and consumer protection?
- What effect do you anticipate in the area of legislation related to portable pensions, transport policy, fuel prices, etc?
- What about employment legislation? Where is the balance of industrial relations? Is it in favour of employers, against closed shops and restrictive practices?
- What is the current policy on training for employment, for young people, for skills and for adults?
- What is the impact of regional imbalances and the response of the national government and the European Community authorities?
- How does the pressure for equality of opportunity and the elimination of discrimination manifest itself?

Figure 14 Environmental Scarring

FACTORS	LIKELY CHANGES	POTENTIAL IMPACT
Political		
Economic		
Social		
Technological		

- What is the influence of European Community institutions on national practice?
- What government departments are particularly relevant to your business? In what areas are they developing policies that should be of interest to your firm? What sections of the European Commission are active in your industry?

If you are unaware of some of the answers to these questions, you should consult your trade or professional bodies, or the government departments concerned.

Economic pressures

- What do the key economic indicators mean for your industry and your company? What about interest rates and inflation?
- What about the exchange rate? Do any of these factors impact on your customers, your competitors, your suppliers?

- What are the unemployment levels like, nationally, in your area, in relation to the skilled people you need in your industry?
- Is your industry growing or declining in employment terms? Is your growth likely to be retarded by a shortage of skilled people?
- Does the movement of workers geographically between employers give rise to implications for housing, pensions, and so forth?
- Who has the spending power now? Older people? Younger people? Private companies? Public institutions? Which government departments have big budgets?

The economic scene is volatile and needs to be constantly monitored. In your planning, you may need to consider how you will deal with alternative economic scenarios. One method of doing this is to put alternative figures (for example, for inflation, interest rates, exchange rates) into your calculations and see what effect they have on, say, cash flow or profitability. This simple technique is sometimes called 'sensitivity analysis' as it enables you to see how 'sensitive' your business is to such variations.

Social pressures

- Do people expect to be involved in decisions which affect their lives? What impact does this have on company communications, negotiations and possible management structures?
- Do people expect an improving quality of life – at work, at home and in the general environment? How will you take this into account?
- How will changing family patterns (for example, higher proportion of divorces and one-parent families, and families where both husband and wife are employed) influence your decisions?
- Will part-time working, short-term contracts, sub-contracting become increasingly important?
- Are people reluctant to move home geographically, and if so, how might this affect your business?

As you can see from this brief list of possible issues, social pressures can influence your business in several ways: the availability and cost of labour, the way you deal with staff, the spending habits and priorities of different customer groups, and so forth.

Technological pressures

- How will the increasingly dramatic improvements in communication methods and systems change the way you work and interact with your customers, suppliers and field staff?

- Consider the all-pervasive impact of new technology: for example, in the home, the factory, the office, the warehouse, the hospital and the retail check-out.
- What will be the effect of improvements in information handling within your firm? What will be the impact on the jobs people do, and perhaps the training they will require?
- How can the dramatic improvements in technological aids for design and control systems be used to your advantage?
- Will developments in biotechnology impact on your business?
- Will methods for improving the efficient use of fuel have a significant effect on your business?

IDENTIFYING THE KEY ISSUES

It is doubtful whether one person can do such an analysis well. If you and a few of your senior managers really know your business, your market-place and what is happening in the world outside, you should be able to do this analysis between you. Do not be afraid to seek information – from your trade body, from the public library, from the relevant government departments.

A good way to gather and sift information is to get each member of the management team to complete a copy of Figure 15 and then to bring all this information together in one document.

This summary document is then circulated to the managers, but with the last column left blank. The managers are then asked whether they agree with the analysis, and if not, to explain why in the comments column.

Bringing this information together in this manner before having a detailed discussion in the management group is much richer and more effective than launching straight into it. An unprepared discussion is less effective, and some people feel inhibited from contributing.

If you intend to apply for financial assistance from a public body you will need to gather background information on its aims and objectives. Normally the assistance will be granted within an operational programme of the body concerned. You will need to find out the objectives of the particular pro-gramme as well as the rules governing financial assistance. Will your applica-tion go to the management board? If so, it is as well to find out about the background of the members so that you can assess how they are likely to view and judge your proposal.

Most of your contact will be with officials. As they are accountable for pub-lic funds you should expect them to be particularly careful about how the funds will be applied and how expenditure will be recorded.

Figure 15 Environmental Impact

FACTORS	LIKELY IMPACT	COMMENT
Political		
Economic		
Social		
Technological		

EVALUATING THE IMPACT

There are clearly too many topics to consider in depth, but you and your colleagues must identify those areas of prime concern to you. You need, therefore, to consider what are the *major* external influences on your industry, and then what are the *main* implications for:

- Your customers and hence your products and services
- Your technology and the way you will work
- The way you will organize your staff and manage your communications and decision-making
- The way you will recruit, train and remunerate your staff

71

Part Three

INITIAL DECISIONS

Chapter 8

IDENTIFY YOUR NICHE

OBJECTIVE: to refine your definition of the business in the light of the scanning exercise so that detailed calculations can begin.

- **List the features of your products and services**

- **Identify the advantages of your products and services**

- **Specify the benefits offered to each group of customers**

- **Consider the ease of serving your customers in each group**

- **Identify your 'USP', your 'unique selling point'**

FEATURES

Having scanned the market-place and identified the particular kind of customers you intend to serve, you must now specify in detail the kind of products and services you propose to provide. In Figure 16 there is a framework to enable you to consider each group of customers. Where will you be 'positioned' in the quality/price spectrum? The price aspect of positioning is covered in more detail in Chapter 9. Here we are concerned with the nature and quality of the goods and services you intend to provide.

If you are talking about a product, what is its size, shape, purpose, power, quality? What power consumption does it require and what plumbing? What floor-space or desk-space does it take up? What size of materials will it take to process? How many items at a time? How automatic will it be? How fast will it go? How much information can it store? Get the idea? List the features of your product.

Figure 16 Market Niche

What is your chosen market niche? Where will you 'position' your goods and services? (Price positioning is covered in the next chapter.)

	LOW QUALITY LOW PRICE HIGH VOLUME	MEDIUM QUALITY MODEST PRICE MODERATE VOLUME	HIGH QUALITY HIGH PRICE LOW VOLUME
CUSTOMER GROUP A			
What can you provide?			
What do your competitors provide?			
What is your competitive edge – your USP?			
CUSTOMER GROUP B			
What can you provide?			
What do your competitors provide?			
What is your competitive edge – your USP?			

If you are making and selling a product, what are the features of the services you provide alongside? What about delivery times? What about minor changes to suit the customer, for example, different colours or minor changes in specification? Can you produce a specially made article to the customer's requirements, or must he or she have a black one, two metres long – or else!

How reliable is your machine? How durable? What about installation, maintenance and after-sales service, spare parts, and so forth? Can it be repaired on site, or be taken away, or must the customer bring it to your plant in the Outer Hebrides? How quickly can you get a service engineer to call? The same day? Next day? Next week – but not on Saturdays or Sundays or after 4.30 p.m.?

Suppose you are offering a service. What are the features of the service? What precisely will you (or your representatives) do? How comprehensive is the service, or are you prepared to do only certain kinds of work? (For example, if you are offering secretarial services, does this include photocopying, word-processing, book-keeping, desk-top publishing, telephone answering?) At what times is the service available? Where can the service be obtained? If you are providing an information service, is this available in written form, with regular updates, on the telephone, with 24-hour availability, via the internet, interactively?

Is there a feature which is inherent in the company, rather than the product? For example, does your company already have a reputation for reliability, quality or personal service? That should be listed as a feature, and moreover, one that might distinguish your products and services from those of your competitors.

Now compare these features with those of the competitors' products and/or services. In what ways do you consider yours is superior, inferior or just plain 'different'? How many of these features will be significant to your customers? How do you know?

ADVANTAGES

Having compared your products and services with those of your main competitors, list what you see as key features of your wares and tick off those which seem to you to offer an advantage (see Figure 17).

You can do this in general terms to begin with. Space is provided for just ten features, but you may draw up your own table and list as many as you wish. Think of your customers as a whole as you do this. Will they like the compact size, the availability of the service at weekends, the rugged construction, the personal touch, the low power consumption, the fast response time? How do you know? This information may come from your own impressions or those of your managers, but are these impressions reliable? Often they are NOT.

Figure 17 Benefits

FEATURES	ADVANTAGES	BENEFITS – CUSTOMER GROUP
List the main features	Tick off the features which offer an advantage	Specify the benefits which you can see for this group of customers

1.

2.

3.

4.

5.

6.

7.

8.

9.

10.

Information of this kind can only be gained by talking to customers – by customer research. If you have not done this research properly, you are building on shifting sand.

BENEFITS

So, you have identified the advantages of your products and services. But do they actually matter to each of your customer groups? What is the benefit to Group A of Advantage 1? If the customers in Group A have plenty of space, a compact design has no particular merit.

What about Advantage 2? If Group B customers do not open at weekends, it is of no consequence. In other words, you need to consider now the requirements of each group of customers and what benefits they can gain by using the products and services you offer. Remember that a benefit is when the customer's life is made easier, or his or her profits increased or reputation enhanced.

SERVING THE CUSTOMER

You must now consider rather carefully just how easy it will be to provide the appropriate level of service to each group of customers. The problem is that each group will have to be reached through relevant advertising media and be serviced according to its own requirements.

You may be tempted to plan for diversification. Be careful. Companies can diversify by increasing the number of product lines or the range of services offered. It is also possible to diversify by increasing the number of customer groups targetted.

Diversification in one or the other direction will add considerably to the burden on management. Can your management team cope? Can your sales team cope? Diversification in both directions is generally a recipe for disaster unless you have more than one self-contained management team.

In recent years formal systems of quality assurance have assumed increasing importance. The international standard (ISO 9000) has been widely adopted by companies who wish to assure their customers that every effort is taken to ensure conformity of criteria for product quality and service levels. Indeed in some markets this accolade is essential for companies wishing to trade. Closely allied to this is the concept of the customer code adopted by organizations that serve the general public.

UNIQUE SELLING POINT

On the basis of all this analysis, you should now be able to come up with what is special about your products and services. What marks you out from the crowd? What are you uniquely offering to your chosen customers?

What is your unique selling point? What is your market niche?

Chapter 9

PRICING POLICY AND PROFIT

> **OBJECTIVE: to review the factors that govern your pricing policy and to determine provisional prices for your products and services as a basis for further calculations.**

■ Calculate your cost –
price – profit relationship
and risk

■ Decide how to take
competitor prices into
account

■ Decide how and when to
apply the cost-plus
method

■ Decide on your market
price

How will you set about setting the prices you charge for your goods and services? The basis of your prices can be:

• What it will cost to produce the goods or to provide the services
• What your competitors are charging
• What the market will bear

For the purpose of discussion, let us call these the 'cost-plus price', the 'competitors' price' and the 'market price' respectively. You will need to use the cost-plus pricing method if you are tendering for a contract against other suppliers, but otherwise it is generally better to offer your goods and services at the market price.

In order to determine the market price you will need to take careful note of your competitors' price, but you do not need to follow their example. If you draw up a price/quality table (Figure 18) you will need to 'position' your goods and services on this table in relationship to your competitors.

Although your prices may not be based on the cost-plus approach, the

Figure 18 Positioning

Where will you 'position' your goods and services? Where are your competitors?

QUALITY =	LOW	MEDIUM	HIGH
PRICE			
HIGH			High quality goods and services can command high prices and good profit margins
MODERATE		Goods and services of moderate quality in the middle price range can generate healthy profits	
LOW	Inexpensive goods and services have a place in the market-place – but profit margins are generally low		

quantity of goods and services you sell at the prices you charge must, of course, cover your total costs and provide you with a profit – a return on the investment in the business.

COST–PRICE RELATIONSHIPS

At first sight this seems quite straightforward. In practice it is not straightforward at all, because the cost of your goods and services depends on how much you actually sell.

There are a number of costs that you incur however much you make and sell up to a certain level. Calculations of costs will be covered more thoroughly later. For now, suppose you are running a bookshop: you must pay rent and rates, heating, lighting, basic wages, the interest on any loans, and so on. You must also take into account the 'depreciation' on any capital items. All these costs are effectively fixed and independent of how much you sell. They are called your 'fixed costs'.

Each book you sell has cost you money to buy. When you sell goods, you must buy more to replace them. The price which you charge the customer for

---

Figure 19 Risk Table

First, estimate the quantity you expect to sell – in the worst possible case you can envisage, what you think is entirely feasible, what you can hope for if all goes well, and a figure which means that the sales are appreciably better than you anticipate – and put these figures in line A.

Next, take your chosen price and multiply up to get the income generated from sales in each case, in line B. Now multiply up your quantity of sales by cost per item to yield the variable cost (line C) and subtract these figures from those in line B to yield the gross profit (line D).

Finally, deduct the fixed cost (line E) from the gross profit to yield the net profit (line F).

A: QUANTITY SOLD	lowest estimate	reasonable estimate	optimistic estimate	highly optimistic estimate
	————	————	————	————
B: PRICE CHARGED × QUANTITY SOLD (INCOME GENERATED)	————	————	————	————
C: COST PER ITEM × NUMBER SOLD (VARIABLE COSTS)	————	————	————	————
D: GROSS PROFIT	═══	═══	═══	═══
E: FIXED COSTS	————	————	————	————
F: NET PROFIT	═══	═══	═══	═══

a book, less the cost you paid for it, represents what is called the 'gross profit'. The more books you sell, the more costs you incur in buying them, so that the costs of purchasing items for sale is variable (it varies with the 'volume of sales'). We call it 'variable cost'.

Every business will have its fixed and variable costs, and there will be some grey areas of 'semi-variable costs' as well. It is important to think this through, as one man's fixed cost may be another man's variable cost. If you are in the publishing business, your fixed costs will be the cost of actually printing and binding an initial print run and advertising the book. In this case, the cost of the books is fixed whether you sell one book or the whole of the 10,000 in your initial print run. The price of each one is a fixed cost – in contrast to the bookseller.

These two examples show that the calculation of costs and profit can be done over a period of time (for example, a month, a quarter or a year of trading in a shop) or on the basis of a specific project, such as the publication of a book. If you are a book publisher, you will need a number of titles to publish over a period of time and you will need to estimate when books will be ready for publication, advertising and selling to estimate what will happen over each period of time.

To see the relationship between the price, costs and profit, draw up your own 'risk table'. Think through your fixed and variable costs and insert these into the table in Figure 19. The table can be used to calculate the risks involved over a period of time or in mounting a project.

Highly simplified examples are provided in Figure 20 to illustrate the principle of the risk table. We noted above that some costs are fixed 'up to a certain level'. This is because a point will be reached where the volume of sales requires extra fixed costs: for example, the shop is too small and needs to be extended, or the number of books sold by the publisher exceeds the first print run and so a decision has to be made whether or not to print more. The shop extension or the extra print run will increase the fixed costs in each case. The effect of this is illustrated in Figure 21.

A brief study of the examples will show that, in theory, a point is reached where the fixed costs must be increased to handle the extra sales. The point at which the gross income is equivalent to the variable costs plus the fixed costs is called the 'breakeven' point. Above this level of sales your business is making a profit: below this point it is making a loss. In Figure 21, the figures in brackets at the bottom of the first column indicate that the business will make a loss at this level of sales.

In this way the risk table will enable you to estimate profit and loss at various sales volumes and price levels. For these initial calculations precise figures are not necessary, but later you will need to do your costing thoroughly to check out this vital equation.

Figure 20 Example Risk Table (Fixed cost unchanged)

A: QUANTITY SOLD	lowest estimate	reasonable estimate	optimistic estimate	highly optimistic estimate
	500	2000	3000	5000
B: PRICE CHARGED × QUANTITY SOLD (INCOME GENERATED) say average £12	6000	24000	36000	60000
C: COST PER ITEM × NUMBER SOLD (VARIABLE COSTS) say average £5	2500	10000	15000	25000
D: GROSS PROFIT	3500	14000	21000	35000
E: FIXED COSTS	14000	14000	14000	14000
F: NET PROFIT/(LOSS)	(10500)	BREAKEVEN	7000	21000

The table is over-simplified, but it does show the basic principles and you should make sure you understand them. Complications include:

- The possibility of getting better discounts from suppliers as your volumes of sales increase, hence improving your profit
- The possibility of offering a variety of products at different prices: you will then need to decide how to allocate fixed costs to different products
- The need to assess at which point your volume of sales will require you to increase your overhead costs
- The need to take into account the taxation implications as they apply to your business
- The possibility of selling your goods in different ways which would make the variable costs more difficult to calculate.

Figure 21 Example Risk Table (Change in fixed cost)

A: QUANTITY SOLD	lowest estimate	reasonable estimate	optimistic estimate	highly optimistic estimate
	500	2000	3000	5000
B: PRICE CHARGED × QUANTITY SOLD (INCOME GENERATED) say average £12	6000	24000	36000	60000
C: COST PER ITEM × NUMBER SOLD (VARIABLE COSTS) say average £5	2500	10000	15000	25000
D: GROSS PROFIT	3500	14000	21000	35000
E: FIXED COSTS	14000	14000	14000	21000
F: NET PROFIT/(LOSS)	(10500)	BREAKEVEN	7000	14000

Bearing all these factors in mind, complete your own 'risk table'.

COST–PLUS CALCULATIONS

From the previous section you can see that fixing price on the basis of cost plus a figure for profit is not that easy in most businesses. It means knowing in advance the volume of sales. Where the technique does come into its own, however, is when you are asked to undertake a particular assignment, whether it be making a product or undertaking a task (for example, contract cleaning or a market survey).

If you find yourself in a tendering situation, you must carefully think through each step of the work you will be offering to do, estimating the cost of the materials, the time taken to do each part, the extent to which you will be dependent on deliveries or work done by other people (including the employees of the customer!), the precise sequence in which tasks will be done and the effect of any possible delays, however caused, on your costs.

You will then need to bear in mind the fact that most jobs can be undertaken at different quality levels. Once you know the cost, you need to add your required profit margin. You will need to determine the quality levels required and then pitch your tender on that basis, hoping that the customer will be prepared to pay your price for the quality you specify, and that this quality/price mix is better than anyone else's. You should endeavour to find

---

Figure 22 Contract Costing (Key Questions)

1. What does the customer want, precisely?

2. On what criteria will the customer decide which tender to accept?

3. What level of quality will you aim at? What delivery time or completion time will you quote?

4. What materials will you need? Where will you get them? What will they cost? How reliable are the deliveries? What are the cost implications of delays here?

5. How long will each step, or each task involved, take to complete? How many hours of work will be involved, and what level of staff will be employed?

6. To what extent will you use sub-contractors? What will they cost? How reliable will they be? What will be the cost implications of delays here?

7. What margin of profit will you require?

out the criteria for the award of the contract and to work within those parameters.

But what has this got to do with planning? When you come to write your plan for an operation of this kind you need to forecast, as best you can, the number and kinds of contracts you expect to win, so that you can work out your cash flow and profit and loss.

Use Figure 22 to stimulate your thinking on typical contracts that will form the core of your business. Make some rough estimates of the costs involved, add in your profit requirement and compare these figures with what customers will be prepared to pay.

COMPETITOR PRICES

As part of your initial survey of the market-place, you should have identified your major competitors, the products and services they offer and the prices they charge. You now need to examine the data more carefully, and to fit them into the price/quality table. Do not be tempted to compete on price alone. This is generally a recipe for disaster, especially for the smaller or medium-sized business.

Large firms have many ways of reducing costs, for example, large runs to reduce the ratio of fixed to variable costs, bulk buying to reduce the variable costs, the use of sophisticated machinery to speed manufacture which can only make sense with large volumes. Furthermore, large firms can sustain particular product lines or services at an unprofitable level to gain a foothold in the market, or to squeeze a competitor – making up for the loss on other product lines or services.

For these reasons you need to be careful in interpreting the data on customer prices, but they are a key factor in the market-place. In general, it is better to compete on some parameter other than cost, for example:

- Quality
- Delivery
- Uniqueness
- Packaging and presentation
- Personal service, tailor made to the customer's need
- After-sales service

Occasionally, a businessperson will consider that his or her product or service is unique and that he or she does not have a competitor. This is very rarely true. If you make an absolutely unique object, it has some purpose. It might be a talking point, a work of art, an implement or a machine. But right now, the likelihood is that your potential customers are living their lives without it! They have other ways to stimulate conversation, other works of art to view, other ways of achieving what your implement or machine will do, although not perhaps so cleanly, or efficiently, or effectively.

But these artefacts are the competition. If your goods and services will do these jobs better, then hopefully people will be prepared to pay. But you may be asking people to move to a different part of the price/quality spectrum, to purchase something in a different 'position' (Figure 18) in the market-place. You need to recognize that, and to overcome people's inertia in accepting new ideas.

MARKET PRICE

By market price we mean the price the customer is willing to pay for the goods and services you are offering, including the quality, frequency, packaging and presentation, after-sales service, financial deal, and so forth. It is for you to determine this, and you should make it as high as the market will bear.

Clearly if the price the market will bear does not give you a profitable return on your investment, you will need to go back to the drawing-board and re-define your business. There is no point in adding a profit figure to your cost and calling this the price when nobody will pay it.

You can only determine this price by a careful study of your potential customers, their needs and their priorities. You must consider how the products and services you are providing meet their needs and respond to their priorities.

Once you have decided on the quality/price position, you must gear your advertising and selling methods to this 'image'. In simple terms, you must manufacture and sell goods and provide services which people feel meets a need which they perceive, in a pleasant, cost-effective manner.

The word 'people' is used deliberately, as it will be people (not 'organizations' or 'companies') that decide whether to buy or not. We return to this question in the sales and marketing sections. Remember that people buy from people they like and to meet a need they perceive.

Your price, therefore, must reflect the benefit that the decision-maker will gain, and be sold on that basis. If your product is for sale direct to the public, for example, will it provide for the purchaser a status symbol to make him or her feel wealthy and successful, or will it help the purchaser to do some tasks that are important (for example, enhancing his or her home, increasing his or her business success) or interesting (enhancing his or her leisure), or will it improve his or her health or appearance?

If not, why should he or she buy it?

Figure 23 Market Price/Quality Factors

Are you selling direct to members of the public?

- Will your products and services enhance their wealth, their self-image, their health, their pleasure . . . or what?

Are you selling to the public through inter-mediaries?

- Will your products and services fit with their existing ranges?
- Will you provide help with merchandising and advertising as part of the deal?
- If appropriate, will you provide installation and after-sales service as part of the deal?
- Are your trading terms acceptable?

Are you selling to industrial, commercial or public bodies?

- Who will make the decision to buy?
- What will be the appeal to the people who will actually use the goods and services?
- What will be the appeal to the purchasing manager of the concern?

Where does your product sit in the positioning table?

What are your competitors charging?

- How do your products and services compare price for price, when you take the overall package into account?

If you are selling your products to a company, the decision-makers will often include the people who will use the materials and services plus the people responsible for actually placing and processing the orders. Here the price/quality position must satisfy both parties.

If you are selling to the public through intermediaries like shops, distributors or agents, then your price/quality position will need to reflect the needs of the public purchaser, but also be acceptable to the intermediaries. Use Figure 23 to summarize your conclusions on the factors influencing price in your particular business.

If you are tendering for a contract you may have a difficult decision to make regarding the price/quality package that will give you the business. Wherever possible you should speak to officers of the company or public authority to determine the actual objectives of the project as well as studying the invitation to tender documentation. This will enable you to make a judgement on the extent to which it is necessary to pare costs to the bone. The alternative is to put forward a realistic proposal that will not only meet the conditions of the 'invitation' but also provide a quality service that will take forward the objectives of the purchaser. It is rarely the best plan to compete on price alone.

Chapter 10

LOCATION AND ADDRESS

> **OBJECTIVE: to review the factors influencing your choice of location, and to decide how many sites you will operate from, what you will do at each site, and list the cost factors.**

- **Define what you will use your premises for**

- **Consider your travel needs and labour requirements**

- **Draw up a specification for your premises**

- **Make decisions about the financial implications**

In deciding just where you will locate your business there are a number of factors to consider (see Figure 24). As you work through this chapter you will be making decisions about the location of the property and its physical condition. Be careful at the same time to make a note of the various costs that are indicated, so that these may be incorporated into the expenses section of your business plan.

PURPOSE

What kind of operation will you be running on your premises? Will there be a retail sales outlet? Sales only to wholesalers or tradespeople? Manufacture? Office work? Bulk storage? Distribution? Will it involve food preparation or the use of dangerous substances?

Where will you site your main office and what will you do there? Will this be a purely administrative centre or will you also conduct your main activities there? Most smaller firms find it better to have their main activities and their 'head office' under one roof. More sites mean more communications by letter

Figure 24 Location

Refer to the text for guidance on completing this schedule.

PURPOSE
- Where will you site your main office?
- What activities will you conduct from this site?
- Will you have any other sites for the business?

(*Note* Complete the next three sections for each site.)

PROXIMITY
- Will your proposed site be near to your customers, or your suppliers?
- What will be the availability of suitable labour at your chosen site?
- Will the location prove acceptable to the managers and skilled people you wish to employ?
- Will your proposed site be near public transport or public roads?

REQUIREMENTS
- Can you obtain planning permission to use the site for the intended purpose?
- How much space will you require?
- How much of this will need to be at ground floor level?
- What services will you require: for example, gas, electricity, water, drainage, telephone, air venting?
- What size vehicles will be visiting your premises?
- What access and egress will you require?
- What parking and vehicle manoeuvring space will you require?

- Will you need to modify the premises in any way, and will your alterations be approved by the local authority and, if necessary, by the landlord?
- Will the premises comply with any legislation relevant to its uses: for example, related to health and safety or to the employment of people there?

FINANCE
- Will the premises be rented, leased or purchased?
- How will you raise the cash needed for the purchase price or premium?
- What will it cost to have the premises properly surveyed?
- What kind of maintenance payments and insurances will you be required to sustain?
- When will the rent and rates be reviewed, and how much should you allow for this in your business plan?

or telephone line (speech, fax or computer network) with the risks of delays and misunderstandings, or movement of people to and fro taking up valuable time. The use of an intranet, and as appropriate the internet, can ease communication problems.

A head office can be sited virtually anywhere that key people are prepared to work. But will you or some of your managers need to visit people (customers, suppliers)? Will you expect to receive customers? If you are running a retail outlet, will you depend on passing trade, or will you expect people to make a conscious effort to visit your store? If you need passing trade, then your premises probably needs to include a ground floor site with a display area fronting on to a high street in a reasonable-sized town. This is expensive, and you must ensure that your turnover and profit levels can sustain the cost.

If yours is a specialist shop, antiques, for example, it might be better sited with other similar shops, as people keen on these objects will usually prefer to come and visit several dealers.

If you want to manufacture or to operate a distribution centre, you will find places (generally out of town and in certain geographical areas) where the costs are relatively modest and where planning permission can be readily obtained.

If you are involved in both manufacture and retail, you may find it necessary to operate from two sites. The questions that follow should be addressed to each of your sites.

You may run a very small business from home, provided that you have the permission of the owner, or the lender if your house is mortgaged. If you do work from home, you must ensure that your business causes no disturbances to the neighbourhood: for example, from extra traffic (deliveries, customers or excessive mail deliveries), noise, dirt, smell or unsightly materials or machinery on public view.

If you have salespeople who operate over areas distant from your main office, you may ask them to operate from home.

PROXIMITY

If you or your senior managers expect to travel a lot, or if you expect many people to visit your premises, then the availability of good road and rail links becomes important. In many businesses the ability to get to your customers quickly is a distinct advantage.

You must also take into account the labour market and amenities in the area where you will locate your premises. Will you be able to recruit and retain good quality staff? If necessary, will you be able to persuade key people to relocate to your chosen area?

Ambitious and able people are no longer content with just a job. They want to live in an area which is pleasant, clean and has amenities for themselves and their families (for example, schools, shops, sports and leisure facilities).

REQUIREMENTS

Once you have decided on the approximate location, you will need to look for a specific site or building, and you will need to draw up a list of your requirements – a *specification*. In the area you have chosen, can you obtain planning permission to use the site for the intended purpose? Does it fit into the structure plan for the area? It might be worth discussing this with a local planning officer and a surveyor. You might find it ueful to look at the internet for further information. Aerial photographs may be available for the area that interests you.

You will need to assess the amount of space you will require for, for example, the storage of raw materials, the manufacturing operation, the storage of finished goods, the office, toilet facilities, maintenance areas, display areas, and so forth. Analyze your operation and estimate your own requirements.

How much space will need to be at ground floor level, for example, as a display area, a sales area, an area where heavy machinery will be sited or stored, where goods will be outloaded?

What services will your operation require (for example, gas, electricity, water, telephone)? Remember that whilst it is not difficult to install gas, electricity and telephones, extra drainage or air extraction systems (for example, for welding operations) may well involve extra expense and time. Will you need higher voltages than the normal mains supply for special machinery, for example?

You will need to consider carefully what vehicles will be visiting your premises. How large will they be? You may use only small vans, but your suppliers may use big vehicles which will need to be able to get close to your loading bay. What access and egress will you require? Will you need to provide parking and vehicle manoeuvring space?

The building you find may not be entirely suitable for your use. Will you need to modify the premises in any way, and will your alterations be approved by the local authority? If the property is rented or leased, will the landlord agree?

If you will be using the premises for certain purposes, for example, food preparation or dangerous operations, or if your work entails the use of dangerous machinery or materials, there may well be special requirements with which you must comply. As people will work there, you will have another set of regulations to consider.

FINANCE

You must decide whether to rent, lease or purchase the property. On the one hand, purchasing a property ties up capital; on the other hand, it might be an investment. That is a matter for judgement, and it is by no means straightforward. Purchasing property will mean that you will not have a landlord to worry about when you make modifications to the premises. In leasehold property, there are restrictions on alterations, and the landlord's consent is generally required.

Whether you lease or purchase you will need to raise funds, and you will need to consider carefully how to do this. In the case of the purchase, the property will often be accepted as collateral for a loan, but not to cover the whole cost.

It is a wise precaution to have the property properly surveyed whether you lease or purchase, even if you intend to occupy only a part of the building.

There are a number of factors to be taken into account when you lease property, and you will need to get sound professional advice on this subject.

You will need to take into account, in your planning, such factors as repair obligations, maintenance charges, user clauses, planning permission, conditions of termination, sub-lets, assignment of lease, security of tenure, the schedule of delapidations, the schedule of condition of the property at the outset, and so on.

You will now have some clear ideas about the location of your premises and the costs. These may include structural survey fees, search fees, premiums for the lease or the purchase price/loan interest, maintenance charges, charges for repairs, insurances, re-instatement at the conclusion of the lease, rent (which may rise substantially on review), rates and the cost of installing services and many structural alterations. All this is quite separate from any furniture, equipment and fittings required.

Part Four

SALES AND MARKETING DECISIONS

Chapter 11

SALES FORECASTING

OBJECTIVE: to make a realistic estimate of your sales over the plan period, to forecast receipts from sales and to set working targets.

- You *must* attempt to forecast sales and revenue

- Take into account any published sales figures

- Take full account of your firm's experience

- Make full use of market survey data

- Contracts require special treatment

- Convert your forecasts into targets

- Use sales forecasts to calculate anticipated revenue

You may consider that it is impossible to forecast your sales accurately. That is probably true, but you *must* try. Your business depends on selling goods and services, and you cannot plan without some idea of how much you will sell, month by month for the first year of your plan, and quarter by quarter for the next two years.

What basis have you got for your sales forecasts?

First, there may be published data on sales for your kind of goods and services. Second, there are the results of your own efforts in the past – if you are already in business. Third, there are the results from your own market studies.

Now use the information from your environmental scan to see what changes are likely to influence this market. Has peace broken out, reducing the market for cables for warships and warplanes? Are there new regulations that make the machines produced by your competitors less attractive? Is there going to be a financial squeeze, reducing housebuilding and the sales figures for 'white' goods? You will know what issues are important to your trade. Now is the time to take these into account.

You must now draw on your own judgement and that of your colleagues in using this data and deciding how much of the market you consider you can penetrate, and how quickly. This depends in part on:

- How well you have identified your market niche, and pitched your prices
- How good you are at reaching your customers and convincing them of the benefits they will gain from your unique selling point
- How much you are blown off course by unexpected activity from competitors or by other factors

Special considerations apply to businesses that operate largely through a limited number of large contracts.

PUBLISHED DATA

In many cases, you can obtain total sales figures for particular types of products: for example, washing machines, video recorders, knitting wool, foodstuff products. It is more difficult to get such data for services, although even here you may be able to find out, for example, the number of television sets or sunbeds hired out.

Even more valuable, if you can get it, is data on sales by particular groups of people (for example, by socio-economic groups). You can obtain data on how many people, in different socio-economic groups, live in particular neighbourhoods; this can prove a valuable guide in, for example, calculating potential sales in a given area for a local shop.

The way you can use data varies according to the business. In siting a shop, for example, you can obtain figures for the turnover for different types of shop in different locations. You can then make a judgement on the likely turnover in the location you have chosen – taking into account such factors as other similar shops, the pattern of local transport and the shopping in the area. In choosing a location, it is not a bad idea to observe the movement of people going past the shop at various times of day and days of the week.

If you are selling products nationwide, then you can often obtain information about total sales, and your work on competitors will tell you who the key players are, and what chances you have of gaining a modest market share. These figures will give you an idea of the volume of sales you might achieve.

If you are opening a restaurant, you need information about how many people eat out, what they spend and what types of establishment they use. You also need some local intelligence about other restaurants in the locality and how well they do. Your sales figures are limited by the facilities (how many 'covers' you have), how much use can be made of them and what hours you propose to open.

In estimating sales in a restaurant, given the above data, there is not really much substitute for actually thinking about how many people you expect to attract into the restaurant, and how much they will buy, each morning, afternoon and evening, each day of the week, each week of the year.

The methods we have described so far are the kind you can use for estimating sales to the public. But if your business is selling machinery or services to business, then you have a different kind of problem. You may be selling only to local firms (for example, secretarial or employment services), or nationally (for example, specialized telephone equipment). Here you need data about the types of firm (in your locality or nationally), and the extent to which they buy your kind of goods or services.

If your business is concerned mainly with gaining a relatively few large contracts, then you need to know how many such contracts are awarded and how large they are.

EXPERIENCE

If you are already in business, then your starting point for estimating sales is clearly what you have achieved hitherto. For the first year of your new plan, write down the sales for each product line month by month that you achieved last year. Note any seasonal variation. Now, based on the kind of arguments used above, anticipate whether your sales of particular products and services will be higher or lower than before. Some people just add ten per cent to last year's figures, but few businesses can ignore changes in fashion and the activities of competitors.

Presumably you are introducing some modified or new products or services. Knowledge of your present customers, their likes and dislikes and future requirements should be a guide to future sales. Ask your salespeople for their views. They should be closest to your customers. If they are not already gathering such information, you should get them to do so in future – in spite of what some marketing experts say!

If you are introducing a completely new group of products or services, but to the same kind of customers, your knowledge of their needs should still be the prime source of the information you use. Here you are probably going to compete with other people who are already established in the market-place, and you will need to undertake your work on the unique selling point and the price positioning very carefully indeed.

MARKET SURVEY

The data referred to in the previous section will have come from your market investigation. But this investigation should also have gathered some data on the kind of customers you seek to serve and the potential sales for your kind of products or services.

If you included these points in your market survey, it should have revealed the extent to which customers would be prepared to use the services you propose to offer. Much of this may not materialize. Competitors may have become more active. In the light of your decisions about your market niche and your price positioning, you should now be able to make some estimates of likely sales. You must now make a judgement on how much you will be able to sell, and how quickly this will build up.

If you are selling nationwide, you will need to assess how effective your advertising will be and what response it will produce. Again, you must anticipate the level of sales you will be able to reach and how fast these sales will build up. If you are proposing to sell through the internet, you will need to understand this enormous, complex and potentially confusing online marketplace. Millions of customers are exploring many thousands of web sites. You will need to know how this market is organized and what action you need to take to optimise the response you generate.

CONTRACTS

If your business is concerned with getting a series of large contracts (for example, for double-glazing new buildings as they are built, designing and managing an advertising campaign or acting as a distributor for a manufacturer), then many of the methods mentioned above will be of limited application.

What you need to know here is how many such contracts are awarded and on what basis. You need to estimate how long it will take you to get your first contract, and how large it will be, then your second and third, and so forth. In this way you can build up a sales projection chart.

If you are selling research services or management consultancy services to public bodies you will generally need to tender for the business. Each body will have its own procedures for processing tenders and you will need to assess your chances of gaining each contract you seek.

SALES TARGETS

Once you have identified what is feasible in terms of sales, these should be written into your plan, not just as forecasts, but as targets for your firm to achieve. If your managers and salespeople have been involved in drawing up these estimates and targets, they will be all the better motivated to achieve them.

Break down your targets by customer profile, by product line or service type, by geographical area and month by month, so that you can see just where you expect the sales to be achieved.

Set out your forecasts month by month for the first year, and quarter by quarter for the next two years, using Figure 25 to record your estimates.

Figure 25 Sales Projection for a Month

You will need a section on each area, for example, North, South, East and West.

AREA N					**AREA S**				
PRODUCTS	1	2	3	4	**PRODUCTS**	1	2	3	4
Sales to Customer					**Sales to Customer**				
Type A	___	___	___	___	**Type A**	___	___	___	___
Type B	___	___	___	___	**Type B**	___	___	___	___
Type C	___	___	___	___	**Type C**	___	___	___	___

FORECASTING REVENUE

Making a sale is good. Receiving the money from the sale is even better! From your knowledge of current practice in the industry, you must now estimate not only when the sales will be made, but also when the bills will actually be paid. In some trades payment is immediate, but in most cases you may have to wait a month, two months or even three months for your cash! Use the method presented in Figure 26 to record when you anticipate making sales, and when you anticipate receiving the cash in your bank account.

Each type of contracting business has its own way of staging payments. Some pay a portion at the outset, then portions as each stage is completed, holding back a portion until the whole work is approved. The staging of the payments must be built into your projection of the revenue to be received.

Naturally if you decide to offer discounts of any kind this must be taken into account in your revenue forecasts. Whichever method you use you should now enter the results in Figure 27 which will provide an essential part of your business plan.

Clearly where you expect cash on the nail, the receipts – in other words, the revenue (for a 'cash sale') – appears in the month when the sale is made; but when payment is expected one, two or three months later, or in stage payments, this must be reflected in the 'credit sales' receipts figures.

Figure 26 Anticipating Revenue

This demonstrates how to anticipate the revenue from sales based on sales forecasts, where payment is expected within one month.

	Month 1			Month 2		
	Sales Volume	Income Earned	Cash Due	Sales Volume	Income Earned	Cash Due
SALES						
Number of units sold (Price per unit = p)	n1			n2		
Income earned		n1 x p			n2 x p	
Cash received			**NIL**			**£n1 x p**

This calculation must be completed for each product or service sold to build up the anticipated revenue expected, month by month for the first year, and quarter by quarter for the second and third years of the plan.

Figure 27 Sales and Revenue Forecast

Month	1	2	3	4	5	6	7	8	9	10	11	12	TOTAL

SALES

Number of Units A
(price of A)
Income from A

Number of Units B
(price of B)
Income from B

Number of Units C
(price of C)
Income from C

Gross Income

RECEIPTS

Cash Sales

Credit Sales

TOTAL SALES

RECEIPTS

Chapter 12

MARKETING STRATEGY

> **OBJECTIVE: to decide on how to reach customers, maintain intelligence about the market-place, secure sales and generate revenue.**

- Decide on how you will attract the attention of potential customers

- Design the message and the medium you need to evoke a response

- Prepare your staff and materials to secure sales

- Prepare to close sales and to follow through

Successful marketing and sales depends on knowing who your customers are – from your previous analysis – and how to reach and influence them. In order to make a sale you must, in simple terms, (a) attract the attention of potential customers, (b) gain their interest in your wares and evoke a response, (c) foster, create if need be, a desire, and focus this desire on the purchase of your particular products and services and then (d) persuade the potential customer to act, in placing an order for which they have the desire, ability and intention of paying! In summary, you need a plan to:

- Attract customers
- Evoke a response
- Focus desire
- Secure action

In order to make a sale you will generally need to start off by reaching a large number of potential customers. As you move from stage to stage in the process, the number of customers often diminishes quite dramatically. Your marketing strategy must take this into account. The drop-out rates from stage to stage depend on:

- Your particular kind of business
- How well you have identified your particular customers
- How well you have adjusted your actions to these customers at each stage

In many instances you will need to reach from 200 to 500 customers to gain a response; of those who respond probably no more than one in ten is really serious, and of those who are serious you will do well to persuade one in three to place an order with you. These are very broad generalizations, but they do represent realistic orders of magnitude in terms of the advertising and sales methods used in all kinds of businesses.

If you can do no better than this, it means that you must reach 10,000 potential customers to make one sale. Have you ever tried to sell an unwanted item of furniture through advertising in a local newspaper? If it has a circulation of 10,000 or more, you stand a chance!

How can you reduce the odds in your favour? The answer is to target your advertising and promotional methods accurately and to streamline the way your firm deals with enquiries.

ATTRACTING CUSTOMERS

It is easy to spend a fortune on advertising which has little impact. List the methods you propose to use to reach your customers. This must be based on a thorough analysis of, for example, what newspapers, magazines and journals they read, what sections of these periodicals they study, what shopping areas they frequent, what exhibitions and conferences they attend, what radio programmes they listen to and (if you can afford this in relation to your products) what television stations they watch. The methods you can use include:

- Paid advertising (newspapers, magazines, journals, radio, TV)
- Press releases, sometimes alongside paid advertising
- Telephone or trade directories
- Mailshots (using your own lists, bought-in lists or agencies)
- Telephone sales calls (your own salespeople or agencies initially)
- Personal sales calls (your sales representatives or agents)
- Displays (for example, a shop or at exhibitions)
- Sales promotions
- Personal contact (for example, at conferences and other events organized by professional and trade bodies)
- Web site on the internet

Whatever method you use, try to build into your plan ways to evaluate its effectiveness: for example, by coding advertisement reply addresses or building a bit of simple research into the questions you ask people who respond and those who ultimately purchase your goods and services.

Use Figure 28 to list the methods you will use, how often you will use them and the costs incurred. Include in this figure any costs incurred in drawing up or purchasing lists of potential customers. Bear in mind that the cost of a good list may be worthwhile if it enables you to target your customers more precisely and to reduce your advertising budget. In the last column, make an estimate of the response you expect to get from each method.

Figure 28 Attracting Customers

In the first column, list the methods you propose to use to reach your customers. Indicate the frequency, for example, of your advertisement or exhibitions (second column), and the cost per month (third column). If this is phased irregularly, make a separate note of the expenditure each month through the first year and quarterly for the next two years. Write down what response (for example, in terms of numbers of enquiries) you anticipate in the final column.

METHODS TO BE USED	FREQUENCY	COST PER MONTH	ANTICIPATED RESPONSE

In some cases, your advertisement or promotion may not, in itself, produce direct responses, but may create an awareness of your products and services, and your existence in the market-place which will make it easier to sell when the time comes. For example, as a builder or a funeral director you may place a regular advertisement in a local paper so that when someone needs your services they are aware of your firm.

EVOKING RESPONSE

The key to evoking a response is to appeal to the vanity or the needs of your potential customer. Do they want to impress the neighbours or get relief for their sore feet? Do they need to create impressive sales documents or get their word-processing done efficiently? Your impact depends on reaching people who feel a need – or who could feel a need if you convey the right message. Only if your firm is well known and has a good reputation among your customers will using its name attract attention.

You need, therefore, a well-designed message and method for prompting a reaction on the part of your potential customers. Why should they stop, as they skim the pages of the magazine, at your advertisement? It is not the aim of this book to go into detail on this subject, but you will need to plan and budget for good design, decide how this will be achieved and what manner of response you will generate (for example, a written reply, a telephone call, a personal call).

The key questions you will need to address to complete this part of your plan are listed in Figure 29. The more specific you are in evoking a response only from the people who are likely to buy, the less time you will have to spend later in weeding out people who will simply waste your time.

FOCUSING DESIRE

The way you react to the customer's response is crucial. Many sales may be lost when someone in your firm answers the telephone in a negative and unconstructive manner. Plan to train all of your people who will have any contact at all with the customers or potential customers. Include the telephonist and the invoicing clerk, not just the telesales people and the sales representatives.

Train your people to ask questions, to take an interest in the enquirer, to seek to help and to meet needs. Where the need can be met by your own products and services, train your people to promote them. Otherwise, your firm should earn a reputation for helping people. Someone once said, 'People buy from people they like'. There is a lot of truth in that. Helping people, even if they do not buy your goods on that occasion, can be very good for business.

Figure 29 Evoking Response

1. What will be the basis of your appeal to the customer?

2. How will this message be put across?

3. What help will you need in designing the advertising and promotional material? How much will this cost?

4. How often will you need to review and revise your design and what will this cost – and when?

5. In what ways do you expect the potential customers to respond?

It is also important at this stage to have a procedure for ensuring that the customer has a genuine desire for the product or services, and the authority or means to pay. If you are selling, for example, machinery or raw materials to a company, you may need to convince two or three different people, so that your strategy must take this into account both in terms of the time your salespeople will need to secure sales, and also the costs involved.

Your plan (see Figure 30) must include a procedure for dealing with enquiries, and for training your people to do this really well. If you are expecting a written response (for example, a completed coupon from a newspaper, or a written request for information or a catalogue), will you send back literature (and if so, what kind?), or will you telephone, or ask a representative to call?

If you expect people to telephone, you will need to train the telephone operator to channel this call quickly to the right person, and that person must be trained to answer the call in a positive, constructive manner, to make a note of all the relevant information, and to arrange for prompt follow-up.

If you are expecting personal callers (for example, at a shop or warehouse, or at an exhibition), you will need literature, and probably samples or materials to exhibit, as well as well-trained sales assistants or consultants on hand.

If you expect a response via the internet, how do you propose to deal with it? Will you have an automatic reaction to an enquiry, or have an operator available at all times, or expect the enquirer to leave a message by e-mail?

Figure 30 Focusing Desire

When your advertising and promotional methods produce a response, how will you deal with it? Do you expect a written, telephone or personal response? What materials will you need to provide (for example, written materials, display materials, specimen products)? What training will your people need? List these below.

RESPONSE ANTICIPATED	MATERIALS REQUIRED	YOUR PEOPLE INVOLVED	TRAINING REQUIRED	COSTS

SECURING ACTION

Sales may be achieved by face-to-face contact, by telephone or simply on the basis of written materials (for example, catalogues and order forms). In each case you need to question why people should buy your products and services rather than those of your competitors.

This means that all your sales and technical literature must stress the help

---

Figure 31 Closing the Sale

1. Will you expect to close the sale by face-to-face contact, by telephone or by written orders?

2. What materials will you need to support salespeople (for example, promotional literature, technical literature, samples, exhibits)?

3. What training will you give to your salespeople?

4. What procedures and documentation will you adopt for recording and progressing orders?

5. How will these procedures be followed through to check on customer satisfaction and invoicing?

6. What information will you collect from potential and actual customers about your advertising and promotion, and about positive and negative responses to your products and services?

7. If you are selling through intermediaries, how will you monitor customer reaction?

---

your customers will receive through purchasing your particular products and services, and your salespeople must be trained to listen to the customer and to respond accordingly.

You will need to plan out the means of recording and processing orders, and ensuring that each customer's needs are met, invoices issued and payment received.

The point of sale contact is ideal for collecting information about how people heard about your products and services, what they found attractive about your advertising and what prompted them to respond. It also provides an opportunity to probe their needs in more depth, providing you with information on which to base the further development of your products and services, as well as clues about how to promote them more effectively. Plan to collect and collate this information.

If you are selling to the public through intermediaries, you will need to work closely with them to ensure that your wares are presented properly. You may need to find alternative means of collecting information about how customers rate your particular products and services, and how they found out about them.

Use the checklist in Figure 31 to record the actions you propose to take.

Part Five

FINANCIAL STRATEGY

EXPENDITURE FORECAST

> **OBJECTIVE: to estimate the expenditure that will be incurred in running the business as a basis for calculating cash flow and profit forecasts.**

- **Calculate what your expenditure will be over three years**

- **Identify and estimate your fixed costs, item by item**

- **Calculate variable costs on the basis of projected sales**

Each possible item of expenditure must now be considered, and in each case you will need to estimate:

- How much it will cost in the first year, the second year and the third year
- When you will be called upon to pay, on a month-by-month basis for the first year, and quarterly for the second and third years

If you feel a need to calculate profit and loss on a monthly basis, you will also need to estimate the cost of the item on a month-by-month basis. Remember that cost is incurred when an item is used or discarded, but expenditure is involved when the cost of the item has to be paid.

It is very important at the outset to recognize the key difference between cash flow (when cash actually comes into the business or out of it – receipts and expenditures) and profit/loss calculations (which are based on the income generated and the costs incurred over a given period or in connection with a particular business activity).

For example, you must pay for raw materials even if you have not used them, but they appear in your profit and loss calculation when they are used, or when they are discarded. In the meantime, if you have borrowed money to pay for the raw materials, then you are incurring the cost of the loan all the time it is outstanding. Any costs associated with the storage of the materials are also ongoing.

When the cost of an item, for example, electricity, is incurred before the bill arrives, the cost is said to be accrued. It is included in the profit and loss, but only appears in the cash flow statement when the bill is paid. The same applies (in reverse) to your pre-payments.

Costs can be broadly divided into:

• Fixed costs, that remain virtually unaltered whatever volume of goods and services you sell
• Variable costs, that actually vary according to the volume of your sales

In some simple businesses the distinction is clear-cut, and the variable costs are directly proportional to the volume of sales. This is generally not the case, however, and there are some items of expenditure which are semi-variable.

Another factor to bear in mind is that fixed costs may change significantly when a particular volume of sales is reached: for example, because you need to employ more staff or purchase more machinery to service the orders. Fixed costs are often called the 'overheads' of a business.

Use Figure 32 as a checklist to prompt you to think about your fixed costs, about every single item of expenditure your business will incur at every stage.

A thorny question is how to deal with inflation. One method is to calculate all the figures at 'today's prices', and expect that as your costs increase so you can increase your prices. The problem is that this will not apply properly to items like depreciation or loan interest payments. If you are dealing with organizations in overseas countries you may need to take into account possible currency fluctuations. (See the section on risk assessment in Chapter 15.)

An alternative method – and one which has considerable merit – is to make a realistic estimate of increases in costs on a year-by-year basis and to estimate how much you will need to increase your prices to cover it.

In preparing these figures it is rarely worthwhile to attempt excessive accuracy. In most cases, figures to the nearest £1 or even £10 will probably be near enough. It is wise to overestimate a little – but not too much – when calculating expenditure.

Figure 32 Fixed Costs – Overheads – For Profit/Loss Calculation

	Year I	Year 2	Year 3
Employees' wages	_____	_____	_____
Employers' National Insurance	_____	_____	_____
Training of staff	_____	_____	_____
Rent (rented premises)	_____	_____	_____
Rates and water rates	_____	_____	_____
Fuel (gas, electricity, etc.)	_____	_____	_____
Telecommunications	_____	_____	_____
Computer running costs	_____	_____	_____
Postage	_____	_____	_____
Printing and stationery	_____	_____	_____
Subscriptions and periodicals	_____	_____	_____
Advertising and promotions	_____	_____	_____
Repairs and maintenance	_____	_____	_____
Insurances	_____	_____	_____
Professional fees	_____	_____	_____
Interest payments	_____	_____	_____
Bank charges	_____	_____	_____
Vehicle and travel costs (other than depreciation)	_____	_____	_____
Depreciation – vehicle	_____	_____	_____
Depreciation – other assets	_____	_____	_____
Other expenses (specify)	_____	_____	_____
TOTAL OVERHEADS	══════	══════	══════

FIXED COSTS

Wages

If you employ people on a regular basis, without taking account of the usual fluctuations in sales, the basic wages of such people (including yourself and your managers) represent fixed costs. If you employ people only when there is work to do, these costs are effectively variable. Furthermore, if any of your employees, for example, sales staff, are paid a commission on sales, that is strictly speaking a variable cost.

Once you have staff, of course, you become liable for their national insurance contributions and to administer their income tax related to their employment with you. In a monthly accounting system the cost will be shown in the month where the employee is employed, but strictly speaking the expenditure should be shown when the employee is paid (net of tax and employee's national insurance), with the related income tax and national insurance normally paid a month later.

List the kinds of people that you intend to employ (Figure 33) during the first, second and third year, and give details of the total number of hours, days or weeks of their employment during each year. This total multiplied by the expected gross rate of pay will give the total wage bill for the year. Ignore employees' PAYE and NI contributions for the calculation of profit/loss. An approximate figure for the employer's national insurance contributions can be calculated on this basis.

Figure 33 Wage Costs

Calculate these figures for each of the first three years.

TYPE OF EMPLOYEE	ANNUAL PERIOD OF EMPLOYMENT	RATE OF PAY	TOTAL WAGES	EMPLOYER'S NATIONAL INSURANCE

Training of staff

Whether you are starting out on a new business or embarking on a new phase in your business, the need to train your staff is paramount. This must not be neglected in your plan. Insert here any course costs and extra travel and subsistence involved – provided this has not been included in the vehicle and travel section.

Rent and rates

On the basis of the property you intend to occupy, estimate the annual rent (if any), business rates and water rates payable. Figure 34 indicates the key questions. Amortization of a lease premium should be included in 'other expenses' (see page 127).

Fuel

On the basis of the property you will occupy and the use you will make of it, estimate the amount of gas, electricity, heating oil, and so forth that you will consume in your business. Ignore fuel for vehicles as this comes under a different heading. Estimate how much you will use each year and the cost incurred for your profit/loss calculation, and note when this expenditure will be incurred.

Do you have any machinery or equipment that has a high rate of fuel consumption? If so, estimate the anticipated total hours of use in one year; and from the fuel consumption per hour and the unit cost of fuel, calculate the total estimated annual fuel cost and when this payment will be due.

Telecommunications and postage

You may well find this very difficult to quantify at first. If you are already in business, you will have past records to guide you, and you will then need to judge whether expenditure is going to be greater or smaller than in the past.

If either the telephone or the postal services are used extensively in your business, then you will need to make these estimates based on your best judgement as to the amounts involved. How many business calls will you expect your firm to make? Over what distance will the calls be made: locally, nationally, in Europe or further afield? What will be the average duration of the calls and at what time of day and rate of charge? From this information, a rough estimate can be made of the annual telephone costs incurred. What use will you make of Facsimile transmissions? Will there be any other telecommunication charges, such as for the internet, including web site?

Computer running costs

Estimate the consumable materials you expect to use over the plan period and when payments fall due. This will normally cover software costs (includ-

Figure 34 Rent, Rates and Water Rates

1. Do you anticipate that leased or rented premises will be required?

2. When will rents be payable (in advance or in arrears, monthly, quarterly or annually)

3. What will be the annual rent payable? Insert this figure in your fixed costs.

4. How long is the contract?

5. When is a rent increase negotiable? If this falls in your first three years it must be reflected in your figures. Seek advice on the likely increase.

6. Will a premium be required? The cost of this must be spread over the contract period and included in the overhead figure for the profit/loss calculation.

7. The time at which the premium must be paid and when the rent payments fall due should be noted for the cash flow in the following chapter.

8. What are the anticipated annual business rate charges? How can payment be phased? How do you intend to pay?

9. What will be the annual water rate charges? How can payment be phased? How do you intend to pay?

ing support costs), maintenance contracts, floppy disks and items for peripheral equipment, for example printer cartridges and inkjet refills. Items such as on-line database subscriptions, computer equipment depreciation and insurance will be covered elsewhere.

Printing and stationery

If this is a minor item, make a rough estimate, based on previous experience if possible. But if this will be a major item of expenditure, you will need to estimate your requirements, including initial stationery supply, letterheads, business cards, complimentary slips, invoices, and so forth, including cost of design and artwork of any logo or heading. Include such items as record books, computer paper and any other special needs.

Subscriptions and periodicals

You will need to include here any subscriptions to trade associations, employers' organizations, professional bodies, and so forth which are important to your business. List any specialist journals, magazines or publications you will require and the cost involved. If you plan to subscribe to an on-line database, include the annual subscription here.

Advertising and promotions

From your marketing plan, you can now estimate the costs of all your advertising and promotional activities, including design and artwork, printing, postage, envelopes, distribution, and so forth. Include any technical leaflets and catalogues under this heading.

Repairs and maintenance

List any machinery and equipment that will require repairs and maintenance. Include also any buildings for which the business is responsible, and any fixtures and fittings. Where you decide to have a maintenance contract, insert this figure in the annual costs, and make a note of when payment will be due.

Where a maintenance contract does not exist, you will need to make sensible provision for repairs and maintenance in your costings and budget. If you have a lease that requires you to reinstate the premises when you vacate it, you may consider it wise to make provision for this cost over the life of the lease.

Insurance

List all of the insurance you will need for your particular business, stating the total amount of cover required and the annual premium. Note whether this will be paid annually or monthly, and during which months. Use Figure 35 to record your estimates.

Figure 35 Insurances

Type of Insurance	Cover Required	Annual Premium	Payment Dates

Professional fees

Decide what professional assistance you will require from a solicitor, accountant, bookkeeper, marketing expert or other kinds of consultant. List the fees you anticipate paying each year in each case.

Interest payments

This heading covers all interest payable on all loans and finance obtained for business purposes: for example, property mortgage, bank loans, hire purchase of equipment and overdrafts (but excluding vehicle finance which is included elsewhere).

In calculating the financing of interest, it is necessary to separate loan payments into (a) repayment of capital and (b) interest. If this is not yet known, then for the first three years calculate interest at the full expected annual rate (APR) on the full amount of the loan: this will be an overestimate, but corrected figures may be substituted when these are known.

It is not possible to include a figure for the interest payable on any expected

Figure 36 Interest Payments

TYPE OF LOAN	AMOUNT	PERIOD	INTEREST ON LOAN	ANNUAL REPAYMENT		PAYABLE INTEREST	(MONTHLY/ QUARTERLY)
			Rate (%)	Capital			

TOTAL ANNUAL PAYMENTS, CAPITAL AND INTEREST   £_____   £_____

overdraft until calculations have been completed on the cash flow. If an overdraft is anticipated, include an estimate at this stage and correct it later. Record your estimates in Figure 36.

Bank charges

These are subject to wide variation and you should check on both the basis of charging and the rates to be charged on your bank account. Based on this and your anticipated use of the account, estimate the annual charge.

Vehicle and travel

Estimate the cost of running each vehicle which you will use in the business. The fixed cost will include depreciation (but see below), road fund tax, insurance, subscriptions to motoring organizations like the AA or RAC, interest on the loan to purchase the vehicles or leasing costs and incidental expenses. The variable costs will include petrol and oil, servicing, tyres, repairs, car-parking fees.

Where the use of the vehicle is not related to the volume of sales, the total annual costs, based on your anticipated mileage, less depreciation costs should be written into the vehicle expenses part of the profit/loss statement, together with any other travel costs, such as air or train fares, hotels, meals whilst on business or mileage allowances.

Figure 37 Capital Expenditure and Depreciation

Prepare a list of all the capital items costing more than £250 that you will need in the first three years. Include buildings but not vehicles.

CAPITAL ITEM	INITIAL COST	ANTICIPATED PURCHASE DATE	EXPECTED LIFE IN YEARS	DEPRECIATION PER ANNUM

Depreciation

The depreciation on vehicles is often accounted for using the 'reducing balance method': in other words, taking a percentage of the net book value at the commencement of the period. Thus the value of a car costing £20,000 would generally be written down at a rate of 25 per cent per annum, giving a depreciation of £5,000 in the first year, £3,750 (25 per cent of £15,000) in the second year, then £2,812 (25 per cent of £11,250) in the third year.

The depreciation on other capital items must be calculated, and also the date on which these capital items will be purchased. Use Figure 37 to record your calculations. If your requirements are complex, you may need to work through Chapter 14 before finalizing this section.

If you purchase and install equipment but cannot use it immediately, for example if you are building up a new plant, you may need to defer the depreciation on these items. Depreciation can start when the plant becomes operational. The funding costs incurred must be accounted for separately.

Other expenses

Include here items such as licence fees and the amortization of a lease premium, together with any other expenses which may be specific to your particular business. Give details in each case.

VARIABLE COSTS

The variable costs will depend very much on your kind of business. We have seen earlier that a fixed cost in one business can be a variable in another. What you must identify is where the cost varies with the volume of sales.

If you are running a road haulage company, for example, your fuel and oil costs will be variable, depending on the loads you carry for your customers. If you are running a retail shop, then the cost of the goods you have *sold* (not the cost of the goods you have bought) represents your variable costs.

Thus, you will need your sales projections to calculate your variable costs. You should estimate total costs for each year. In addition, you will need to think through when you will actually have to pay for these variable items. This is explained in Chapter 15.

Chapter 14

CAPITAL EXPENDITURE AND LIQUIDITY

OBJECTIVE: to review the capital expenditure needs of
the business and alternative ways of meeting this
expenditure whilst retaining adequate liquidity.

■ **Review the capital items
you require**

■ **Recognize the need for
liquidity**

■ **Itemize the sources of
cash available**

■ **Review key financial
ratios as you plan**

■ **On this basis, plan your
investment strategy**

REVIEWING REQUIREMENTS

You have already drawn up a preliminary list of the capital expenditure
requirements of the business in Chapter 13, in Figure 37. We now need to
examine this list in more depth and to decide how these capital items should
be funded.

List separately:

• Property
• General plant, equipment and machinery
• Fixtures and fittings
• High-tech equipment that quickly becomes obsolete
• Motor vehicles

Figure 38 Financing of Capital Items

Prepare a list of all the capital items costing more than £250 that you will need in the first three years. Include buildings and vehicles.

Indicate in each case whether the article will be purchased outright or subject to a loan, rented or leased.

CAPITAL ITEM	INITIAL COST	ANTICIPATED PURCHASE DATE	METHOD OF PAYMENT	COMPLETION OF LOAN OR END OF LEASE

Your major investment will probably be in buildings and in complex machinery. You may also need to invest in a variety of furnishings and fittings and maybe in vehicles. In drawing up the profit and loss reports for limited companies the accountants use some well tested methods for assessing depreciation.

However, when you are assessing the viability of your business, you are not limited to these conventions. If you recognize that a computer will need to be replaced very quickly or become obsolete, you can write it down more quickly in calculating your business viability.

It is a matter for judgement and discussion with your accountant whether you use the 'straight line' or the 'reducing balance' method for calculating depreciation.

If you have a lot of spare cash available, you may wish to use this for capital items to reduce your need for borrowing cash, particularly during periods when interest rates are high or uncertain. However, as we shall see in later chapters, there are occasions when a business needs to raise ready cash and it is very unwise to tie up all your funds in capital items which cannot readily be converted to cash.

You should keep a proper record of capital items purchased. You will need this to keep track of depreciation costs and to deal with the tax authorities. Each year you will need to compile a statement of the current book value of your assets by category, clearly showing the depreciation you have allowed in each case. If these assets are likely to change significantly during the year it may be advisable to produce a summary statement or schedule of assets by categories on a quarterly basis. If for example, you expect to purchase additional vehicles during the year, the value of this asset category will change significantly.

LIQUIDITY

This need for ready cash is referred to as 'liquidity'. Cash in your hand or in the current account at the bank is 'liquid' – it can flow quickly. If your money is on deposit, it may not flow quickly, except at an unacceptable price. Such funds are less liquid.

Funds which are tied up in buildings, plant and equipment cannot usually be released quickly. Funds used to purchase stock items, or tied up in work in progress, can only be realized quickly if the items in question are highly saleable.

Finished goods can often be turned quickly into cash – unless the market has become saturated or the fashion has changed. Often, however, finished goods sold quickly do not fetch a good price.

SOURCES OF FUNDS

In essence, there are three ways to secure funds in a company for use in current expenditure or in capital items, and you will probably end up with a combination of all three methods. These ways are:

- To use money which belongs to the *owners* of the business (equity funding), which may come from original investments by the owners, or from profits generated by the business and retained in the firm rather than being distributed to the owners
- To use money which is effectively *loaned* to the company, whether this is in the form of a formal loan (for example, a mortgage, hire purchase agreement, bank loan or overdraft) or as goods which have been delivered to the company, but where a period of time elapses before payment falls due (in other words, credit from suppliers)
- To lease, hire or rent, for example, machinery, vehicles, property

You may be able to apply for a grant for public funds, for example from a government department or agency, or from an international body. There are a number of grants available through directorates or agencies of the European Union.

It is important to distinguish between these sources of funds. The owner invests in a business to gain a return on that investment, to make a profit which can be used either to develop the business or to be taken out as dividends or bonuses. The business could, however, make a loss, so that the owners are worse off, financially, than they were before. The owners have the last call on any money in a business (the government, lenders and employees all come earlier in the queue), and so can face a loss as well as a gain. They have taken a calculated business risk.

A lender expects to be paid interest, and to receive back the amount loaned (the 'principal' or capital originally loaned) in due course. The lender expects to be paid, in full, on time, whenever a payment falls due, and certainly takes precedence over the owners if funds are in short supply.

The ratio of *lenders' money* to *owners' money* in a business is crucial, and as a rule of thumb it should rarely exceed one. This ratio is known as the 'gearing' of a company. A highly geared company, where the ratio is much higher than one, is regarded by many people as potentially insecure.

When a firm borrows money from the bank there are a number of different mechanisms that can be employed, but two common methods are the term loan and the overdraft. Generally speaking, the term loans are used for capital items, whereas the overdrafts are used to cover current expenditure (in other words, to help with the 'buffer'). Banks can generally call in overdrafts if they wish, and it is unwise to become overly dependent on this method of funding.

If you consider that your company can apply for a publicly financed grant there are three things to consider.

1. Can you conduct your business in a way that enables you to meet the criteria for receiving grant aid?
2. Will the way you use the funds help the granting body to meet its objectives? Meeting the grant criteria may enable you to receive the award in the short term, but helping the grant-awarding body to achieve its goals may help to secure ongoing support.
3. Are you prepared to pay the price that may be involved? This could include the time taken to negotiate for the grant (in duration and management effort), the possible restriction to your freedom of manoeuvre (you must continue to conform to the grant criteria), and the need to keep detailed financial records that enable you to account to the awarding body and organizations that regulate public funds.

Often there are limits on your ability to move cash between budget sub-headings. The technical term for this movement is 'virement'. This may mean that you cannot move public funds from, say, administration to travel costs, or capital items to expenditure, without specific permission. Capital assets purchased from public funds frequently remain the property of the grant-awarding body. This may mean, for example, that you cannot sell a building or change its use. Funding you receive from a European body may be channelled through your own government. That means that technically your accounts will be subject to inspection by the national auditing body as well as by the European auditing body and the grant-awarding body. (This is, of course, in addition to your responsibilities to the taxation, customs and national insurance collection agencies. You must also ensure that you conform to government accountancy and reporting regulations.)

Cash is needed in a business to purchase capital items, but it is also required to act as a 'buffer' between payments which are due to the company and payments which are due from the company. A study of your trading cycle throughout the first few years could reveal a need for substantial cash for this 'buffer', and without it, you could technically become bankrupt. Indeed, you are more likely to fail in business through a shortage of cash than through low profitability.

At this stage, complete Figure 39 so that you have a clear picture, in a very simplified way, of where the money in the business has come from, and how it is being used. From these figures you can calculate the gearing ratio.

KEY FINANCIAL RATIOS

There are three other factors to consider. What is the ratio of the money you owe to the money which is owed to you? If your debts are much greater than the money owing to you, this is helping to fund the business – but may be damaging your reputation! On the other hand, if you are owed much more than your debts, you are effectively funding someone else's business.

The second factor, and one which is very important for planning purposes, is the amount of stock you hold, whether this is in the form of raw materials, work in progress or finished goods. Keeping a lot of stock means using storage spaces, tying up capital and, if for any reason it becomes obsolete or unfashionable, entailing problems.

For these reasons you need to plan for the minimum stock levels which will enable you to run your business effectively (Chapter 16). The manufacturing method known as 'Just in Time' has been adopted by a number of companies as a way of minimizing stock and work in progress.

The third factor is the liquidity ratio. What proportion of the funds can be

---

Figure 39 Sources of Funds

On the left hand side, list the funds being used in the business. As this will vary from time to time choose a particular date. For example, if you are in business it could be the end of your financial year. If you are starting a business this should be the day on which you propose to start trading, and the position you anticipate at the end of the first year.

On the right hand side, indicate how your total funds have been used under various headings.

Owners' money originally invested.	Tangible assets, property, plant and machinery, vehicles.
Loans from various sources.	Raw materials, work in progress. unsold finished goods.
Profits from previous years (if any).	Money owed by debtors.
Money owed to creditors.	Cash in hand or in the bank.
Grants from external bodies, if any	

These two sides should balance, indicating how the business is funded and enabling you to calculate the gearing ratio (lenders' money divided by owners' money). If you have purchased capital items out of grant you need to be clear about whether these items belong to the company or whether the grant conditions mean that these are technically the property of the awarding body.

---

readily converted into cash to pay bills? This has been discussed above, but now is the time to do some sums and ensure that you are planning for a stable business.

FURTHER FUNDING

If further funds are needed, there are three avenues to explore:

• To invite others to invest in the business; to become joint owners with

you and to join in the venture, putting their own money at risk alongside yours, providing you do not mind losing a share of the business
- To raise a loan or overdraft facility, providing you retain a healthy liquidity and gearing ratio
- To sell capital items you own, if this is possible at a reasonable price, and to lease them instead

You can now choose between these alternatives in the light of your needs for liquidity, for appropriate gearing and the debt to creditor ratio you are aiming for in your business.

If you plan to run a tight ship, you will need to plan in firm controls and sound information systems (Chapter 20).

Chapter 15

PROFIT FORECAST AND RISK

OBJECTIVE: to calculate the level of profit (or loss) anticipated on the basis of the assumptions made so far about the business, and to apply sensitivity analysis to the data as a basis for refining decisions.

- ■ **Calculate anticipated gross and net profit (or loss)**

- ■ **Consider alternative scenarios as you prepare your plan**

- ■ **Calculate the 'risk' involved if your sales volumes are low**

- ■ **Use sensitivity analysis to assess alternatives and make decisions**

When preparing the financial estimates for the profit/loss calculation, it is important not to lose sight of the ultimate objective: to produce realistic figures which can be used as the basis of decision-making now. Although one must estimate the expenses under the various headings as carefully as possible, it is often impossible to be really accurate.

It is time consuming to complicate the planning exercise by trying to be too precise. For most planning purposes, it is preferable to work in round pounds (ignoring the pence) for the figures inserted into the list of expenses and the projected sales income, otherwise you might fail to see the wood for the trees. It is, therefore, recommended that to maintain clarity pence are not entered, and that figures should at least be rounded off to the nearest pound, and in many cases, to the nearest five or ten pounds is often sufficient.

If you are able to use a computer to prepare your estimates, you may do so; but if the figures are not too complicated, it is better to use a pencil and paper. It is all too easy to get the computer to do sums for you without realizing the full significance of what is happening, and sometimes this causes you to forget the assumptions that are inherent in your figures (and hence the areas of doubt).

Many people find that actually writing down some of the key numbers and where they come from gives them a 'feel' for the figures and how they relate to one another – a 'feel' that few people get from computer print-outs. If you can use a calculator, you will find this a great help – especially the kind that prints out all the numbers you have entered in and adds up the number of entries.

If there is some doubt about the total amount that may be anticipated under any heading, it is preferable to err on the higher side rather than the lower. Do not grossly overestimate as this could mislead you into a wrong decision.

CALCULATING PROFIT – OR LOSS

In a straightforward business the 'gross profit' is calculated by taking the income generated by sales from the variable cost associated with these sales. Multiplying the sales forecast figure in units (say SF1 units for year 1) by the price charged (say PC1) gives the forecast of income generated from sales $(SF1 \times PC1)$. Multiplying the same sales forecast figure by the unit variable cost (VC1) of sales yields the variable costs $(SF1 \times VC1)$ associated with this sales volume.

Variable costs are discussed in Chapter 13. These are costs which relate directly to the volume of goods sold and generally this relationship is direct proportionally. Thus in this simple case, doubling the sales volume will double the variable costs.

However, we have the fixed costs to take into account. These were calculated in some detail in Chapter 13 and you can take the estimate prepared in Figure 32 for this, and calculate the total profit as shown in Figure 40.

When the gross profit is equal to the fixed costs the business has made neither a profit nor a loss. This volume of sales is called the 'breakeven point'. Clearly, below this volume of sales the business makes a loss, and above it the business is making a profit. Strictly speaking, we should also take into account any other income which the company has received, as shown in Figure 41.

Taxation rules change from time to time and you will need to take professional advice on the effect of National Insurance and Value Added Tax on your level of profit. You will also have to pay tax on profit, and this tax will be calculated according to the rules prevailing at the time. The Inland Revenue has its own method for calculating the profit on which tax should be levied.

There are some other terms and concepts you may find useful. The term 'markup', commonly used in the retail trade, denotes the amount of gross profit that is added to the cost of the goods to arrive at the selling price, often

Figure 40 Profit and Loss Forecast

	Year I	Year 2	Year 3
SALES FORECAST: units sold @ price per unit of P1...			
GROSS TURNOVER (quantity × price)			
Less: variable costs			
Gives GROSS PROFIT			
Less: OVERHEADS from Figure 30			
NET PROFIT/(LOSS)			

This ignores any income from other sources, for example, interest from bank deposits or from the sale of assets at prices above their 'book' value. No account is taken of tax on profit.

expressed as a percentage. Thus, the cost of goods purchased plus percentage markup = selling price.

Another term which is used is the 'gross profit percentage', which is the amount of gross profit expressed as a percentage of the selling price. Thus, the gross profit on an item divided by selling price × 100 = gross profit percentage.

For example, a product with a selling price of £100, which costs £70, gives a gross profit of £30 (i.e. 30 per cent), but a markup of 42.9 per cent.

RISK ASSESSMENT

The element of risk can arise in a number of ways and in your plan you will need to identify possible risks and how you intend to deal with them. After reading this section, make a list of the kinds of risk relevant to your business. Against each item indicate, in general terms, what action you propose to take at the outset, if any, and what you can do if the unwelcome event occurs.

Figure 41 Profit and Loss Forecast

	Year I	Year 2	Year 3
SALES FORECAST: units sold @ price per unit of P1...	═══	═══	═══
GROSS TURNOVER (quantity × price)	───	───	───
Less: variable costs	───	───	───
Gives GROSS PROFIT	═══	═══	═══
Plus other business income	───	───	───
TOTAL	───	───	───
Less: OVERHEADS from Figure 30	───	───	───
PROFIT/(LOSS) (before tax)	═══	═══	═══

Remember that tax on profit will be deducted according to the Inland Revenue rules.

Some risks are insurable. For example, at the outset you might take out an insurance policy against a fire in your warehouse. Bad debt risks can be reduced by investigating the credit-worthiness of your key customers. However you may not be able to take action at the outset to deal with eventualities such as difficulties in securing raw materials or severe unexpected transportation problems. If you have taken out loans you must consider the way that interest rate changes might affect your business. Changes in the law may affect your business, especially if you are trading overseas. Trading with overseas customers or suppliers also means that currency fluctuations must be taken into account. Nevertheless, it is necessary to try to foresee such eventualities and to indicate in your plan how you would cope if these things were to happen. One way of getting a good list might be to involve your key managers in a 'brainstorming' session. When you have finished this exercise it can form a section in the 'special factors and risk assessment' part of your plan.

Risks associated with late payments will be dealt with in the next chapter, but you must face the possibility that some customers may never pay up.

Although you have done your best to forecast your sales figures, it is rare for these to be totally reliable. We need to be able to assess what will happen if you fail to achieve these targets. One way to get a grip on this problem is to calculate profit or loss based on more than one sales figure. You might, for example, calculate these figures on the basis of the worst sales you can imagine, the sales you consider you should reach reasonably easily, an optimistic figure and sales that were exceptionally good (see Chapter 9).

If we ignore other sources of income for a moment, we can see that the relationship between these key figures (volumes of sales, selling price, variable unit costs and overheads) can help us in our planning. Consider the information in Figure 42 where we are choosing to take four possible sales figures. By inspection you can see the breakeven point and the effect of sales volumes above and below this figure. You should now be able to substitute your own figures, estimating your worst possible sales figures for the first year, the most likely figure, an optimistic figure and a wildly enthusiastic overestimate!

Figure 42 Risk Calculation

Sales volume	50 Units	100 Units	200 Units	500 Units
@ £25 each sales income	£1,250	£2,500	£5,000	£12,500
Variable cost @ £5 each	£250	£500	£1,000	£2,500
GROSS PROFIT	£1,000	£2,000	£4,000	£10,000
Less the fixed cost	£2,000	£2,000	£2,000	£2,000
NET PROFIT/(LOSS)	(£1,000)	BREAKEVEN	£2,000	£8,000

You will now be able to assess the business risk inherent in your plan. You can now see the full implications of your decisions about the fixed costs you plan to incur, the sales volumes you anticipate, the cost of your materials and the chosen selling prices for your wares. Are you satisfied with the level of profit anticipated? Is it really worth investing that much money (the owners'

Figure 43 Sensitivity Analysis (Reduced overhead)

These figures illustrate what happens when the overhead is reduced by 25 per cent.

Sales volume	50 Units	100 Units	200 Units	500 Units
@ £25 each sales income	£1,250	£2,500	£5,000	£12,500
Variable cost @ £5 each	£250	£500	£1,000	£2,500
GROSS PROFIT	£1,000	£2,000	£4,000	£10,000
Less the fixed cost	£1,500	£1,500	£1,500	£1,500
NET PROFIT/(LOSS)	(£500)	£500	£2,500	£8,500

The breakeven point is reached with only 75 units sold and the loss at 50 units sold is much reduced when the overhead is reduced by 25 per cent.

money, as originally invested, plus retained profits – Figure 39) to earn that level of profit?

An external investor would compare the return on capital employed in your business with the figures other firms achieve. How will you stack up? Another ratio to look at is the net profit in relation to turnover. Is that good enough?

In the first year of trading you may not be able to reach an adequate level of profit, but you then have to look at the second and third years (and beyond if necessary) to see when reasonable levels of profitability will be attained, and make your decisions on that basis.

It is on this basis that potential investors or lenders will look at the business plan, and the senior people you can trust in your firm should understand the issues involved.

Quite often when this point is reached, you may conclude that the profit level and risk is unacceptable, and the next step in planning is to consider your options. What are they?

Figure 44 Sensitivity Analysis (Reduced variable costs)

These figures illustrate what happens when the variable unit costs are reduced by 20 per cent.

Sales volume	50 Units	100 Units	200 Units	500 Units
@ £25 each sales income	£1,250	£2,500	£5,000	£12,500
Variable cost @ £4 each	£200	£400	£800	£2,000
GROSS PROFIT	£1,050	£2,100	£4,200	£10,500
Less the fixed cost	£2,000	£2,000	£2,000	£2,000
NET PROFIT/(LOSS)	(£950)	£100	£2,200	£8,500

The breakeven point is reached with 96 units sold and the loss at 50 units sold is slightly reduced when the overhead is reduced by 20 per cent.

ALTERNATIVE SCENARIOS

You can look first at the overhead figures. Are there any areas where savings can be made without serious loss to the business? Could you manage with less expensive furniture and fittings for the first few years? Could you do with fewer telephones, less space, or storing your goods in a less expensive location? You may have to look more carefully at your advertising budget. Does it relate realistically to your sales volume and the income you expect to generate?

A second area for examination is the variable cost per unit of sale. Can you find a cheaper source of supply? Is there a less expensive method of distribution (if this is part of your variable cost)?

Finally, are you sure you have fixed your price realistically? If you are determined to produce good quality goods and services, you will want to buy in

Figure 45 Sensitivity Analysis (Increased price)

These figures illustrate what happens when the selling price is increased by ten per cent.

Sales volume	50 Units	100 Units	200 Units	500 Units
@ £27.50 each sales income	£1,375	£2,750	£5,500	£13,750
Variable cost @ £5 each	£250	£500	£1,000	£2,500
GROSS PROFIT	£1,125	£2,250	£4,500	£11,250
Less the fixed cost	£2,000	£2,000	£2,000	£2,000
NET PROFIT/(LOSS)	(£875)	£250	£2,500	£9,250

The breakeven point is reached with only 89 units sold and the loss at 50 units sold is materially reduced when the selling price is increased by 10 per cent.

---

good raw materials and do the job properly. If so, then are you still trying to compete on price? Or can you realistically increase your price a little?

SENSITIVITY ANALYSIS

With the information at hand you can readily calculate what happens in each case. Using our simple example (Figure 43), reducing the overhead by 25 per cent will mean that we reach the breakeven point more quickly (at 75 units of sale) and our risk of losing money is considerably reduced.

By reducing the variable unit costs by 20 per cent (Figure 44), the breakeven point is reached with 96 units sold and the loss at 50 units sold is slightly reduced. When the selling price is increased by ten per cent, the breakeven point is reached with only 89 units sold and the loss at 50 units sold is materially reduced (Figure 45).

Now it is your turn to assess the effects of variations in either your overhead expenses, your unit variable costs or your selling prices.

You will need to consider carefully the way in which costs vary with volume. For example you may find that at a certain point you can buy raw materials at a lower cost, decreasing your unit costs. On the other hand you may reach a point where you need to invest in new plant and equipment and your overheads increase. In both cases this will influence the breakeven point and you will need to take such factors into account.

Once you have finalized your decision, these are the figures to put into the final plan.

Chapter 16

TURNOVER AND STOCKS

> **OBJECTIVE: to determine the stock levels to be maintained in the company in the light of the anticipated turnover levels, so that you can assess the impact on requirements for capital employed in the business and cash flow.**

- **Determine the levels of raw materials you intend to hold**

- **Decide on the levels of finished goods you need to have**

- **Plan for the level of work in progress**

- **Estimate the total capital employed, on average, in maintaining stocks**

If you are a manufacturing company, the likelihood is that you will need to buy and store raw materials and partially made-up goods for use in the factory. You also have plant and equipment and you will wish to carry some essential spares.

If your manufacturing process involves a number of steps, you will need to produce partially-made items and some of this 'work in progress' will be stored, albeit temporarily. Finally, you may have a modest store of finished goods ready to supply to your customer. Retailers and wholesalers also hold stocks of finished goods bought in and ready for sale.

If machinery spares form a significant proportion of your stockholding, prepare a similar chart to that in Figure 46 so that you can estimate the costs involved. If you are running, for example, a farm machinery maintenance business, the cost of holding spares can be quite high.

The costs associated with all this storage includes the cost of the capital tied up in the business (and this can materially reduce your profits) and also the cost of the storage space. If some of your goods are perishable or sensitive, you may need to control the environment in the store, for example, in respect of temperature, humidity or atmospheric gases – a further cost factor. Pest control can be a problem in some trades. If stocks are high, you also run the risk of having the goods left on your hands if the lines become unpopular for any reason, or if the goods deteriorate.

You will need to examine the level of stocks required at each stage, taking into account: the need to maintain a range of goods for sale; the speed at which you can make the goods; and the speed and reliability of deliveries. In the case of bought-in goods, you will need to specify how often you will order new supplies. (You may find that bulk orders give you a better discount, but do not be tempted to plan to do this if this causes you to hold unacceptable levels of stock.)

Record your decisions in Figure 46 and use the figures to calculate the capital to be employed in the business to maintain these stock levels. Is this acceptable? Have you allowed for this level of storage capacity? Will you need to revise your capital plans?

Relevant figures will also be used for the profit/loss calculation. For cash flow purposes you will also need to determine the amount of stocks you intend to secure at the outset, and how these are to be built up during the first year of trading, on a month-by-month basis, reflecting your sales projections.

Figure 46 Levels of Stock

RAW MATERIALS

ITEM	STOCK LEVELS (minimum)		STOCK LEVELS (average)		RE-ORDER		
	Quantity	Value (£)	Quantity	Value (£)	Frequency	Quantity	Value (£)

TOTAL AVERAGE VALUE OF RAW MATERIAL STOCKS HELD £_____

WORK IN PROGRESS

ITEM	STOCK LEVELS (minimum)		STOCK LEVELS (average)	
	Quantity	Value (£)	Quantity	Value (£)

TOTAL AVERAGE VALUE OF WORK IN PROGRESS HELD   £_____

FINISHED GOODS

ITEM	STOCK LEVELS (minimum)		STOCK LEVELS (average)		RE-ORDER (if this is appropriate)		
	Quantity	Value (£)	Quantity	Value (£)	Frequency	Quantity	Value (£)

TOTAL AVERAGE VALUE OF FINISHED GOODS STOCKS HELD   £_____

If your business is in retail you have a slightly different problem. In some cases the public will be willing to inspect samples and wait for products to be made to order. Generally, however, in the retail business you need to purchase and have in stock products that you believe you can sell to the public. Selling space is expensive and you may need an off-site storage warehouse for goods you wish to bring into the shop quickly. You will have the added problem of seasonal variation in sales. You may find it helpful to draw up a table of goods you intend to hold in the retail outlet and goods you intend to have in a warehouse. Once again you will need to take into account lead times for obtaining goods. In your accounting procedures and estimates you will need to allow for a proportion of goods that you may need to write off or sell at a knock-down price.

Chapter 17

FORECAST CASH FLOW

> **OBJECTIVE: to forecast when money will flow into and out of the business so that the firm will always be in a position to pay its bills and manage its cash flow efficiently.**

- **Note the structure of the cash flow forecast sheets**

- **Estimate your receipts**

- **Estimate your payments**

- **Calculate your requirements for cash and make adequate provision**

You forecast your firm's expenditure in working through Chapter 13 and the anticipated income from sales of your goods and services by the methods indicated in Chapter 11. As we have seen (Chapter 14) there are also other sources of income to the business (for example, owners' investments, loans, asset sales, interest on bank deposits).

A major planning and management tool is a sheet which shows, month by month, how much money is flowing into the business, and how much is flowing out. Note that we are dealing here with the actual movement of money, not placing or receiving orders, moving goods or using fuel.

If we compare these headings with the profit/loss forecast, we will find important differences which we need to examine and understand. These arise because the profit/loss calculation is concerned with linking income from sales with the expenditure incurred in providing them, whereas the cash flow is concerned with movements of money which will not be 'in phase' with sales or the consumption of supplies, and so forth.

STRUCTURE

You will notice from Figure 47 that down the left hand side we have first of all the opening balance and list of sources of income, followed by expenditure headings.

Figure 47 Headings in the Cash Flow Forecast

MONTH	0	1	2	3	4	5	6 ... 12	TOTAL

RECEIPTS

Opening balance (B)

Owners' investment
Loans from . . .
Cash sales
Credit sales
Asset disposals
Interest received

TOTAL RECEIPTS (R)

PAYMENTS

Premium on lease
Purchase of property
Purchase of plant,
   furniture and fittings
Purchase of vehicles

Raw materials
Goods for sale
Employees' net wages
Income tax and NI
Training expenses

Rent (rented premises)
Rates and water rates
Fuel (gas, electricity, etc.)
Telecommunications
Computer running costs
Postage

Printing and stationery
Subscriptions and periodicals
Advertising and promotions
Repairs and maintenance
Vehicle and travel costs
 (exclude vehicle purchases)

Insurances
Professional fees
Loan repayments
Bank charges
Bank interest
Value Added Tax
Other expenses (specify)

TOTAL PAYMENTS (P) _____

RECEIPTS LESS PAYMENTS
FOR THE MONTH (M) _____

**CASH REMAINING IN
THE BUSINESS (C)** _____

If this is a plan for a new business, you may well require some cash transactions before you actually start to trade. If so, the state of play anticipated before trading should be summarized in the column for Month '0'. Ignore the opening balance for Month 0, and insert, as appropriate under receipts, how much money you expect to be paid into the business up to that date, for example, by the owners or from loans.

Under the payments heading, indicate any items you want to purchase before trading commences (for example, property, plant and equipment, stationery, raw materials) or bills you expect to pay (for example, telephone installation, insurances). For the new business, subtract the payments from the receipts for the pre-trading period to give the opening balance for Month 1.

If your business is already trading, ignore the Month 0 column and carry forward the opening balance (in other words, what you expect to achieve by the starting date of the planning period) to the top of Month 1.

In Month 1, make a note of any further receipts you expect to receive, for example, from cash sales. Then work carefully through each item of expenditure and predict the level of payments you anticipate for that month.

The receipts less payments for the month will yield the net income for the month (M = R − P). If you add the opening balance, this will indicate how much cash is left in the company at the month's end (C = B + M). This figure C for Month 1 becomes the opening balance for Month 2, and the process is repeated.

In the final column (headed 'total') you may care to add together the rows and subtract payments from receipts as a cross-check on the arithmetic. It will also help in the preparation of your budgets as it will indicate what you expect to spend on each item of expenditure during the year, and how much income you actually expect to receive during the period (as opposed to the income you have earned).

If you are operating as a limited company you will need to make provision for the payment of corporation tax and you will need to add a column for this. The law on advanced corporation tax is particularly complicated and you may need to take special advice on the dates when payment will be required.

If you are trading as partnership or as a sole trader you will need to account for tax (and national insurance) on profits personally. This may be paid from the business account provided it is clearly shown as 'drawings'.

If you are trading in more than one currency you may need (a) to maintain your main records in one currency, and (b) to add one or more columns where you record the value of relevant items in the 'trading' currency for that item. You will generally be required to express your official accounts in the normal national currency and to use specified rates for reporting purposes.

RECEIPTS

You will need to consider carefully at what stage it is necessary to call on the owners' money and loans. If your business has any surplus assets (for example, equipment) these can be sold to generate cash. Although in the profit and loss account such a transaction will appear as the difference between the sale price and the 'book' value, in the cash flow forecast you will record *all* the cash you expect to receive.

Month by month, for each of the 12 months of the first year of the plan, insert the cash you expect to receive from sales and interest on deposits, and any other sources of income.

Later we shall examine whether this will be enough, and if not, study the options available.

PAYMENTS

Estimate payments, in the month they will fall due, for any purchases or services used: for example, for plant, equipment, raw materials, goods for sale, rent, rates, water rates, gas, electricity, telephone, printing and stationery, subscriptions, periodicals, advertising and promotion expenses, repairs, maintenance contracts, vehicle costs, travel and subsistence costs, insurances, professional fees, loan repayments, bank charges and bank interest payments (where these are not part of a loan repayment).

You will note that in the cash flow forecast, payments for raw materials and other variable costs are shown when they are made, not when the materials are bought, or used, or sold as part of the finished article.

Note that employees' wages are paid net of tax and insurance: the employees' tax and National Insurance, plus the employer's National Insurance contributions are paid in the following month. If you intend to make a contribution to the employees' pension fund, make allowances for this.

In dealing with loans, it is necessary to distinguish between the interest payments and repayment of capital; but in the cash flow forecast, all we are concerned with is the amount of money actually paid out, on a month-by-month basis.

How you deal with postage is a matter for you to decide. You can record what you expect to spend on postage or, as many firms do, you can use an 'imprest' system for postage (and also for minor items of expenditure). If you use an imprest system, you can record the cash you will use to initiate and to top up the imprest.

Under the heading of training expenses you can record either the course costs, or the course costs plus the participants' travel and subsistence costs.

The list of headings may not quite fit your business, although it should cover most eventualities. If you do not require some of these headings, leave them out. You may need more: for example, if you employ any subcontractors, you will require an extra line to make a note of what payments will be due to them, and when.

IMPLICATIONS AND DECISIONS

When you have completed the first year, study carefully the bottom line, and make a note if the figures drop below zero (in other words, if the receipts plus opening balance expected in the month is less than the payments due). We sometimes call this a 'negative cash flow'. Such figures often appear in the forecast for the first year of trading when the initial calculation of the cash flow is completed.

You cannot leave the plan in that state as it implies that when that month is reached the firm will be unable to pay its bills. You must review your funding structure to ensure that, by one means or another, you will be able to meet your commitments.

If, on the other hand, the bottom line is always in surplus, and a substantial surplus for some time, you need to plan to use this cash in some way, even if you simply put a proportion of the sum into a high interest account.

A negative cash flow can become serious very quickly if, for example, your debtors pay you very slowly but your creditors demand payment promptly. If you anticipate this, you must make provisions for dealing with it. You may be able to accelerate payments by offering discounts for prompt settlement of bills, or through factoring – provided your business can bear the costs.

ALTERNATIVE PRESENTATION OF DATA

Some funding organizations require a summary of balance sheet movements on a quarterly basis. This presentation (referred to by some people as a type of cash flow forecast) will show how the firm's sources and application of funds have changed with respect to a specified reference date. This will quickly indicate, for example, how the firm's capital is tied up in plant and machinery, or work in progress has changed during the period. It will also indicate the cash available. See the section on liquidity in Chapter 14, and the discussion of the balance sheet in Chapter 18. See Figure 48 for a typical format for this method of presentation. For the larger operating company this is particularly useful for senior managers: it presents a view of cash resource movements uncluttered with detail.

If this is a new company, the reference date may be taken as the day on which trading begins. For an existing company the date will normally be the beginning of a particular accounting period. These figures will then correlate with the balance sheet for the end of the previous trading period.

In this presentation account is taken of the depreciation of capital items, making clear the basis used for depreciation (Chapter 13). The value of stock, raw materials and work in progress is normally taken as the lowest of (a) the cost and (b) the current market value. Care must be taken in drawing up and interpreting this table. A higher debtors figure, for example, could be due to slower payments or increased sales. A higher figure for finished goods could be a reflection of higher production or lower sales. A transfer between stock and sales will incur no actual cash transfer until the relevant invoice is paid.

Figure 48 Quarterly Summary of Balance Sheet Movements

	1st Quarter	2nd Quarter	3rd Quarter	4th Quarter
FIXED ASSETS				
Buildings				
Plant				
Furniture				
Vehicles				
Computers				
Other				
CURRENT ASSETS				
Raw materials				
Work in progress				
Finished goods				
Debtors and prepayments				
LIABILITIES CAPITAL				
Equity (Owners)				
Retained profit				
OTHER LIABILITIES				
Loans				
Tax				
Creditors and accruals				
NET CASH				

Note: The figures represent the difference between the current values and the values at the 'reference date'. Bad debts are taken into account in the Debtors and prepayments. See text for interpretation.

Chapter 18

FUNDING REVIEW

OBJECTIVE: to review funding provisions for the business in the light of the capital and cash flow requirements estimated.

- **List the assets and liabilities of the firm**

- **Review your capital requirements**

- **Draw up balance sheets based on your forecasts**

ASSETS AND LIABILITIES

From the information you have gathered to underpin your plan, you are now in a position to draw up a balance sheet at the outset of the first year and at the end of the first, second and third years. The balance sheet at the end of the first year is, of course, the opening balance sheet for the second year. See Figure 49 for a simplified balance sheet: as you will see it is closely related to the source of funds work sheet (Figure 39) we saw earlier.

A balance sheet is a list of all the assets (what the firm owns) and liabilities (what the firm owes). These assets may be:

- Fixed ('permanent' assets like land, buildings, plant, machinery, furniture, fixtures and fittings)
- Current ('short-term' assets like stocks, debtors, cash and petty cash)
- Intangible (assets like customer relationships, patents, know-how which have a value but no physical existence)

On the liabilities side we have the investors' capital, because the firm owes it to the investor! Similarly, the business is, in effect, being funded by money owed by the firm to Her Majesty's Inspector of Taxes and other creditors, as well as money owed to the bank (term loan or overdraft).

Figure 49 Simplified Balance Sheet

LIABILITIES			ASSETS		
Capital (owners' money)			**Fixed assets**		
Owners' investment	£60,000		Buildings	£95,000	
Retained profit	£90,000		Plant	£50,000	
		£150,000	Furniture	£25,000	
					£170,000
Deferred liability			**Current assets**		
Term loan		£50,000	Stocks	£45,000	
			Debtors	£30,000	
			Cash	£5,000	
					£80,000
Current liabilities					
Creditors	£20,000				
Tax liability	£5,000				
Bank overdraft	£25,000				
		£50,000			
		£250,000			£250,000

If you expect to receive funds from a public body, study the conditions of the grant carefully. You may find that capital items purchased with this money become the property of the awarding body. In this situation make this clear in your accounts and maintain a separate asset list.

You will need to take care in the way you present receipts from grant-awarding bodies. A grant for a building may be shown as a reduced cost and this will have an effect on your depreciation. A grant towards labour costs will effectively reduce the revenue costs of wages.

PREPARE BALANCE SHEETS

From your previous work you will now know what funds are required for buildings, plant and equipment, furniture, fixtures and fittings and also the

Figure 50 Balance Sheet (Commencement of year)

LIABILITIES		ASSETS	
Capital (owners' money)		**Fixed assets**	
Owners' investment		Buildings	
Retained profit		Plant	
		Furniture	
		Vehicles	
		Computers	
		————	————
Deferred liability		**Current assets**	
Term loan	————	Raw materials	
		Finished goods	
		Debtors	
		Cash	
			————
Current liabilities			
Creditors			
Tax liability			
Bank overdraft			
	————		————
	════		════
	————		————

cash required to pay bills (from the cash flow forecast).

Complete Figure 50 based on your previous work in Chapter 14 (for capital items, especially Figure 38) and in Chapter 17 (for cash injected into the company and items purchased which become assets). Assets purchased at the outset of the year depreciate as described in Chapter 14, so that they have lower 'book values' at the end of the year. Complete a similar balance sheet for the end of the year.

Examine these balance sheets, and take careful note of the key figures and ratios. Consider, for example, the following questions:

- Are the firm's assets planned to grow or decline?
- Is the firm soundly geared or is the ratio of other people's money to the owners' money too high?
- Is the ratio of debtors to creditors reasonable?
- Are the stock levels approximately right for this operation?
- Is the level of 'working capital' high enough?

The 'working capital' in a business is calculated by subtracting the current liabilities from the current assets. The composition of the working capital will fluctuate between the different items, notably between stock and cash, but the level must be high enough to cope with these fluctuations. An indication of the level required will be given by the cash flow forecast.

REVIEW CAPITAL REQUIREMENTS

This is a suitable point at which to review the consistency of your overall financial strategy. The opening and closing balance sheets must be consistent with the anticipated profit/loss and the cash flow. Take some time to check out some of the key items (see Figure 51). Capital assets such as buildings, plant, furniture, vehicles and computer equipment do not give rise to cash flow movements during the year unless they are bought or sold. Related costs, for example for maintenance or related loans, are accounted for elsewhere. These items will reduce the profit level by depreciation during the period and hence also reduce the final balance sheet figures. Items such as raw materials will be bought during the year. The profit is reduced by costs incurred in ordering these, but the cash flow occurs when payment is made for them. Similarly a profit is generated when an item of finished goods is sold, but cash flows only when you receive payment. A series of simple sums should enable you to ensure that for each balance sheet item the opening and closing balances are consistent with the cash flow forecasts and profit/loss calculations.

In the light of this information, you may wish to review the way your firm is to be funded. If you decide you may have insufficient cash, you can:

- Seek more investment from owners
- Take out a further term loan
- Ask for an overdraft facility from the bank
- Consider leasing, renting or factoring
- Review your expenditure plans

Figure 51 Financial Consistency

Initial Balance Sheet	Effect on Cash Flow during period	Effect on Profit/Loss during period	Effect on Final Balance Sheet
Assets			
Buildings			
Plant			
Furniture			
Vehicles			
Computers			
Raw materials			
Work in progress			
Finished goods			
Debtors			
Liabilities			
Owners' investment			
Retained profit			
Term loan			
Creditors			
Tax liability			
Bank overdraft			
Cash available			

Part Six

PUTTING IT TOGETHER

Chapter 19

REVISE YOUR PLAN

OBJECTIVE: to bring together the various elements of the plan and to combine these into a coherent whole.

- Decide on your business name, address and mission statement

- Review the 'people plan' and your marketing strategy

- Ensure cohesion between the various financial elements of the plan

- Satisfy yourself that it is realistic and practical

Name of the business

What thought have you given to the name you will use to describe your business? It is often very difficult to decide, and you need, of course, to check that someone else is not already using the one you want. You will probably need to talk to people with ideas and with people in your firm – the working group you set up at the outset.

Does the name that you have decided upon sit well with your kind of business? Will it help to create the right 'image' – or be misunderstood or a hindrance?

Address of the business

The location of your business has been explored in Chapter 10. Presumably you will trade from your premises and this will be your 'business address'. In most cases this will present no problems. The only question to ask is whether this address itself creates the right 'image', but that will not be an issue in most kinds of business.

You can, of course, use a Post Office Box Number, and this is often employed by mail order companies who wish to discourage personal callers.

Nature of the business – mission statement

Your original draft from the work on Chapter 4 now needs to be brought out, examined and discussed by your working group. In the light of revisions to your plan, for example, in respect of the customers you hope to serve or the goods and services you propose to offer, does this need to be revised?

At this time you may be in a position to take this statement and, with the support of your key people, rephrase it as a 'mission statement', worded in a manner calculated to inspire confidence in your customers, ambition in your staff and managers – and fear among your competitors.

If you are hoping to receive financial support from public funds it might be worthwhile making sure that your business name sounds respectable and sound. It might be worth checking this out in any of the languages spoken in the countries where you wish to trade. When your name appears in the annual report of the granting body it should not look unduly out of place!

People in the business

As your business idea has been refined, you may have cause to revise your assessment of the skills you will need to succeed (Chapter 5). This may mean that you have to look again at the people in your business, their strengths and weaknesses, and any further training they may require.

Are there any special requirements for qualified staff to run your particular business? You should check this out and ensure that you have staff with the requisite qualifications if any of the occupations relevant to your business are regulated: for example, in travel agency management, civil aviation, taxi services or transport management.

Now is the time to look again at your recruitment policy. If you will need more employees, spell out the people you will need, how you will recruit, select and train them. You may also need to reassess what help you will need from external experts.

Marketing and sales strategy

Work on the profit/loss projections and on the cash flow forecasts may have led you to revise your sales forecasts, or your advertising and promotion methods, or even your pricing policy and market niche.

If so, you must re-visit your marketing and sales strategy (Chapters 11 and 12) and make the necessary revisions now. You must also ensure that your plans for marketing and selling are consistent with your mission statement (your revitalized statement about the 'nature of the business').

Profit/loss forecasts

Were your initial calculations satisfactory, or did they lead you to make adjustments in your business plan? You should, at this stage, bring together on one set of papers all the information about the profit/loss forecasts for the three years, as in Figure 52.

Are these current figures final, and do they reflect a potentially healthy trading position? Are the assumptions realistic and achievable?

Figure 52 Summary Profit and Loss Forecasts

	Year I	Year 2	Year 3
SALES FORECAST: units sold	═══	═══	═══
@ price per unit of P1 . . .			
GROSS TURNOVER (quantity × price)	___	___	___
Less: variable costs	___	___	___
Gives GROSS PROFIT	___	___	___
Plus other business income	___	___	___
TOTAL	___	___	___
Less: OVERHEADS from below	___	___	___
PROFIT/(LOSS)			
(before tax)	═══	═══	═══

OVERHEADS/FIXED COSTS

Employees' wages	___	___	___
Employers' National Insurance	___	___	___
Training of staff	___	___	___
Rent (rented premises)	___	___	___
Rates and water rates	___	___	___
Fuel (gas, electricity, etc.)	___	___	___
Telecommunications	___	___	___
Computer running costs	___	___	___
Postage	___	___	___
Printing and stationery	___	___	___
Subscriptions and periodicals	___	___	___
Advertising and promotions	___	___	___
Repairs and maintenance	___	___	___
Insurances	___	___	___
Professional fees	___	___	___
Interest payments	___	___	___
Bank charges	___	___	___

```
┌─────────────────────────────────────────────────────────────┐
│  Vehicle and travel costs              ─────    ─────    ─────│
│     (other than depreciation)                                 │
│  Depreciation – vehicle                ─────    ─────    ─────│
│  Depreciation – other assets           ─────    ─────    ─────│
│  Other expenses (specify)              ─────    ─────    ─────│
│                                                               │
│  TOTAL OVERHEADS                       ═════    ═════    ═════│
│                                                               │
└─────────────────────────────────────────────────────────────┘
```

Cash flow forecasts

In Chapter 17 the method for drawing up the cash flow forecast for the first year was explained. You should now complete this exercise by working out a cash flow forecast for years two and three in your plan, but on a quarterly basis (see Figure 53 for guidance).

Figure 53 Cash Flow Forecasts (Second and third years)

	SECOND YEAR				THIRD YEAR			
QUARTERS:	1st	2nd	3rd	4th	1st	2nd	3rd	4th
RECEIPTS								
Opening balance (B)								
Owners' investment								
Loans from . . .								
Cash Sales								
Credit Sales								
Asset Disposals								
Interest received								
TOTAL RECEIPTS (R)								
PAYMENTS								
Premium on lease								
Purchase of property								

Purchase of plant,
    furniture and fittings
Purchase of vehicles
Raw materials
Goods for sale
Employees' net wages
Income tax and NI
Training expenses

Rent (rented premises)
Rates and water rates
Fuel (gas, electricity, etc.)
Telecommunications
Computer running costs
Postage

Printing and stationery
Subscriptions and periodicals
Advertising and promotions
Repairs and maintenance
Vehicle and travel costs
    (exclude vehicle purchases)

Insurances
Professional fees
Loan repayments
Bank charges
Bank interest
Value Added Tax
Other expenses (specify)

TOTAL PAYMENTS (P) _____

RECEIPTS LESS PAYMENTS
FOR THE MONTH (M) _____

**CASH REMAINING IN
THE BUSINESS (C)** _____

Are you confident that you have identified all sources of income and when the cash will flow, and all items of expenditure and when they are due for payment? Have you made adequate provision to cover your cash needs throughout the plan period? You may find it useful to prepare a quarterly summary of balance sheet movements (see Chapter 17).

Capital expenditure plans

Are you satisfied that you have correctly identified all items of capital expenditure? Have you decided, in the light of your work on cash flow forecasts and the funds available, when each item will be purchased? Have you decided upon the method you will use for calculating depreciation?

Stock purchasing policy

Have you carefully considered your stockholding policy in relation to raw materials, work in progress and finished goods? Have you determined your purchasing policy and the quantity of goods you will order at a time?

Figure 54 Outline Business Plan
(Key questions)

NAME OF THE BUSINESS
Does this now fit the nature of the business?

ADDRESS OF THE BUSINESS
Is this location suitable?

NATURE OF THE BUSINESS
Does this statement match with your current thinking?

PEOPLE IN THE BUSINESS
Have you identified the key skills needed for success and how you will ensure these are available to the business?

MARKETING AND SALES STRATEGY
Is this consistent with your 'nature of the business' statement? Will it work?

PROFIT AND LOSS FORECASTS
Are these healthy, based on your current assumptions?

CASH FLOW FORECASTS
Have you identified all sources of income and items of expenditure, and when they will occur? Have you made sure that you can cover your needs?

CAPITAL EXPENDITURE PLANS
Have you identified all items of capital expenditure and how you will fund them?

STOCK PURCHASING POLICY
Have you decided upon the level of stock to keep, how much you will start with, and in what quantities you will re-order?

FUNDS REQUIRED – FINANCIAL BASE
Have you satisfied yourself that you have a firm financial base?

BOOKKEEPING – MANAGEMENT INFORMATION SYSTEMS

SPECIAL FACTORS AND RISK ASSESSMENT

ACTION PLAN – KEY DECISIONS – TARGET DATES

Are all these decisions correctly reflected in your profit/loss projections and in your cash flow forecasts? Have these levels been taken into account in your work on 'working capital', and on the level of capital employed in the business?

Funds required – financial base

Have you identified the sources of funds available to the business and the use to which these funds will be put? Have you properly considered renting or leasing where appropriate? Have you determined your anticipated gearing? Are you satisfied with the financial base of the firm and with projected balance sheets through the period?

Other factors

We shall be considering the methods you will use for bookkeeping and managing information in Chapter 20. You will need to consider now whether there are any special factors which relate to your business (for example, licences, patents, copyright) and what actions you will need to take to ensure that these are put in hand. (See also the section on 'People in the Business' above.)

MANAGEMENT INFORMATION

OBJECTIVE: to decide, in broad outline, the information systems you will use to manage the business, including your bookkeeping system.

- Identify your needs for management information

- Plan to monitor sales and keep in touch with your market

- Plan to manage your money

- Plan to manage your people

In any business you need to manage your marketing, your money and your people. This means putting in place sensible means of setting targets and collecting and collating data to enable you to keep track of progress.

This book is not a treatise on management or on management information systems, but at the planning stage much of the information you produce can, with a little thought, be used as the basis of management control systems and incorporated into the plan.

MARKETING AND SALES DATA

The sales forecasts you have prepared and decided to include in your plan (Chapter 11) must now be turned into targets. You will need to divide up the year into months, and set out what you hope to achieve by way of sales of each product or service you provide. A simplified chart is provided in Figure 55 to illustrate the kind of documentation you can use, based on the sales forecasts.

You will notice that the price is also mentioned alongside each product. If you find it necessary to offer any discounts, it is important to record this information alongside each product line or type of service. The effect of discounts should be included in your plan.

Figure 55 Monitoring Sales

SALES	MONTH =	1		2	
		Forecast	Actual	Forecast	Actual
Number of units A					
Price					
Income from A					
Number of units B					
Price					
Income from B					
Number of units C					
Price					
Income from C					
Gross income					
RECEIPTS					
Cash sales					
Credit sales					
TOTAL SALES					
RECEIPTS					

If you have a number of lines, you should work out the monthly gross profit per item of each line, and from this, the contribution to the overhead made by sales of each product line. You will recall that the firm only moves into profit when the total gross profit exceeds the overhead. Thus, in each month you can calculate the total gross profit by adding the figures for each line.

Then you will need to plan a system to record the orders placed, goods and services delivered, invoices issued, payment received, and so forth. Thus,

Figure 56 Monthly Contribution to Profit

Table I Use to calculate the contribution to profit from each line

MONTH =	1		2	
SALES	Forecast	Actual	Forecast	Actual
Number of Units A
Price				
Income from A
Less variable cost				
CONTRIBUTION TO PROFIT (A)				

Table II Add up the contribution to profit from each line

MONTH =	1		2	
GROSS PROFIT	Forecast	Actual	Forecast	Actual
Line A
Line B
Line C				
TOTAL				

your monitoring system will be an extension of your sales forecast documentation.

At the same time you should plan to collect information about the marketplace. This should certainly involve collecting information about your customers, who they are, what they buy from you, how often and in what quantities, what they like about your products and services, what related goods and services they are interested in having, how their own businesses are developing, and so on. You should be able to collect much of this data through your sales force. Where this information is not readily available, plan to collect it and add the costs to your plan.

If you have a significant proportion of repeat business, you will need to set up a system for recording your dealings with each customer. From your financial systems (see below) you should be able to keep your actual dealings on file, but your recording system should also contain 'soft' information about each customer as described above, and a record of any comments made, significant telephone conversations and visits.

If you expect to receive grant aid you should monitor the 'political' situation, the environment within which the grant-aiding body operates. A change of government or a change in policy could influence the aims and objectives of the grant body. You may need to take this into account to secure ongoing support.

FINANCIAL INFORMATION

The financial information you will need depends on the nature of the business; but two crucial factors which are common to all types of firm are *cash flow* and *profitability*.

The cash flow forecast sheets you have prepared provide a simple, but effective, monitoring tool by providing two columns for each month (as in Figure 57). The first column will contain your forecast figures, and the second the actual receipts and payments made. You will need to customize this table to meet the needs of your own organization. The kind of detail provided in Figure 57 provides a useful basis for preparing departmental budgets. Heads of departments should draw up their own budgets from a zero base (see Chapter 1), listing in each case the assumptions they have made in building up the figures. As time passes each head of department should be able to account for differences between the forecast and the actual figures on the basis of the changing situation. This data will point up areas for improvement.

For planning purposes cash flow forecasts are produced on a monthly basis, but if your cash flow is precarious you may need to monitor this on a week-to-week, or even day-to-day, basis.

It may be useful to compile a summary of balance sheet movements on a quarterly basis (see Chapters 17 and 19). For senior managers this data provides valuable indicators of the state of the business – especially the way capital is being used in respect of raw material, work in progress, finished goods, and the figures for debtors and creditors.

As you manage the business you will find it useful to update the forecasts from time to time. Some organizations undertake this task on a quarterly basis, and where they have the computing power, the cash flow forecasts are updated monthly. This is particularly valuable if the trading pattern renders the firm vulnerable to a cash shortfall, for example if large amounts of cash flow frequently into and out of the business.

As mentioned above you will need a sound system for following up orders to ensure completion, invoicing and follow-up to ensure payment.

Taken together, this information will provide the basis for drawing up a bookkeeping system that will keep track of your income and expenditure, allocate each item to appropriate subheads that can be used for cash flow and profit monitoring, budget control and management information. Many computer-based systems exist and it should not be too difficult for you to find one appropriate to your needs. Make sure that you, and your key people, understand the system, and that it provides you with what you want: (a) to manage the business, and (b) to account for your activities in financial terms.

Figure 57 Monitoring Cash Flow

MONTH =	1		2	
SALES	**Forecast**	**Actual**	**Forecast**	**Actual**
Opening balance (B)				
Owners' investment				
Loans from . . .				
Cash sales				
Credit sales				
Asset disposals				
Interest received				
TOTAL RECEIPTS (R)				

PAYMENTS

Premium on lease
Purchase of property
Purchase of plant,
   furniture and fittings
Purchase of vehicles

Raw materials
Goods for sale
Employees' net wages
Income tax and NI
Training expenses

Rent (rented premises)
Rates and water rates
Fuel (gas, electricity, etc.)
Telecommunications
Computer running costs
Postage

Printing and stationery
Subscriptions and periodicals
Advertising and promotions
Repairs and maintenance
Vehicle and travel costs
   (exclude vehicle purchases)

Insurances
Professional fees
Loan repayments
Bank charges
Bank interest
Value Added Tax
Other expenses (specify)

TOTAL PAYMENTS (P)

**RECEIPTS LESS PAYMENTS
FOR THE MONTH (M)**

**CASH REMAINING IN
THE BUSINESS (C)**

PEOPLE INFORMATION

If you employ people, you will need to keep appropriate personnel records; but managing people involves much more than that. It involves ensuring that they are aware of their responsibilities and resources, that they are trained and guided in carrying out their duties, that they have clear aims and objectives.

It also involves letting people know how they are doing, giving praise and rewards as appropriate and keeping them informed and consulted on matters which affect them. Your key group of managers should be involved, as far as possible, in drawing up your plan, in formulating the assumptions on which it is based, and in making the crucial decisions.

Be careful, in managing people, to select measures of performance which go beyond what can be measured in figures. A full discussion about managing people is outside the scope of this book, but is covered by other books by the same author, including *How to Manage People* (Hutchinson Business Books, 1984), *Profits Through People* (Hutchinson Business Books, 1990) and *Perfect Teamwork* (Arrow Business Books, 1995).

OTHER DATA

According to the nature of your business you will need to establish monitoring systems, for example, for your stores, capital items, and so forth. In each case bear in mind the purpose of the record.

On the one hand, you have responsibilities to keep records so that you may deal with the authorities (for example, income tax, National Insurance, customs and excise, health and safety matters, licensing bodies). If you expect to receive a grant from a public body, make sure that your accounts will enable you to satisfy the requirements of the funding body and the organizations that regulate or audit the finances of that body. But for the day-to-day management of the business you need to provide information for your managers and your staff which will help them to make better decisions.

Chapter 21

COMPLETE YOUR PLAN

OBJECTIVE: to prepare the written document known as the business plan, setting out the relevant parts in order.

- Assemble your working papers ready for the final task

- Collate sections on the business name, address and mission statement

- Pull together sections on people, marketing and sales

- Check that the financial sections are consistent and clear

- Set out your 'critical path analysis' as a guide to decision-making

ASSEMBLE YOUR DATA

If you have worked carefully through the chapters, you will have far more information than you need to include in the formal plan. This information was needed to prepare the plan, and will be valuable as you put the plan into effect, and as you seek to explain it to, for example, senior staff, investors or lenders.

The work you and your colleagues have put into the plan will also be of enormous value if any unforeseen factors arise. The knowledge you now have will enable you to recognize the implications of the new situation and help you to make your decisions.

However, it is not wise to clutter up the written plan with too much detail. What is wanted in most cases is the summary sheets of key data with text to explain how it all fits together. All the supporting information should be carefully filed away. If you have to answer questions, for example, from investors, lenders or senior staff, you may well need to refer back to these supporting papers.

In this chapter we shall review what should be included in your formal written plan. In most cases, the text and financial tables can be simply assembled from the work you have done.

Name of the business
Address of the business
Nature of the business – mission statement
These sections are straightforward and have been discussed in detail in earlier chapters, especially Chapter 4 (Figure 10) and Chapter 19.

People in the business
- Describe the key people in the business and explain how, between them, they have the necessary skills to ensure success
- Describe any steps you propose to take to enhance the skills of your key people
- Describe any recruitment you propose to undertake, and why you consider the people you need will be available in the labour market
- List any outside expertise you require and how you propose to meet that need

Marketing and sales strategy
This should set out:

- Your customers, and what evidence you have about them
- What products and services you will offer
- How you will reach your customers, your advertising and promotion
- How you will engage with your customers and secure orders
- How you will maintain market intelligence

Profit and loss forecasts
Forecasts of the profits for each of the three years must be presented with full supporting information about income and expenditure, and explanations of all assumptions made. Figure 52 provides a model for presenting this financial data.

Cash flow forecasts
Full month-by-month forecasts of receipts and payments should be presented for the first year, and quarterly forecasts for the second and third years. Provide notes to explain each key section, and any arrangements that have been or will be made for, for example, loans, overdraft facilities or leases. A model format is provided in Figure 47.

Capital expenditure plans

A copy of Figure 38 with accompanying notes is required.

Stock purchasing policy

An account of your plans based on Figure 46 with explanatory notes should suffice.

Funds required – financial base

You will need to list here the sources of cash in the business and how these will be used to fund capital items and working capital. This is explored in Chapter 19.

Bookkeeping – management information systems

All that is required is a note outlining the key areas you propose to monitor, and the methods you will use, as discussed in Chapter 20.

Special factors and risk assessment

List here any special requirements (for example, licences, approval of premises, planning applications, qualified people) and the steps you plan to take to meet them. Outline the key risks and how you would expect to deal with them.

Action plan – key decisions – target dates

Set out here the timetable for action. Consider every action you need to take. Make a special note of actions which must occur in a particular sequence: for example, you need to refurbish a building before you can furnish it and occupy it.

Make an estimate of how long each step in the process will take. Figure 58 is an illustration of one way to plan ahead. The example, highly simplified, assumes that you have found a suitable shop and know that it is in a sound condition. You plan to open the shop.

Figure 58 Critical Path Analysis (Simplified form)

Note Activities which lie on a vertical line can all start at the same time. The next decision cannot be taken until the action which takes the longest has been completed.

For example, after the 'START', arranging finance takes only four weeks, but obtaining planning permission takes ten, so that the premises cannot be purchased until the ten weeks have expired

---

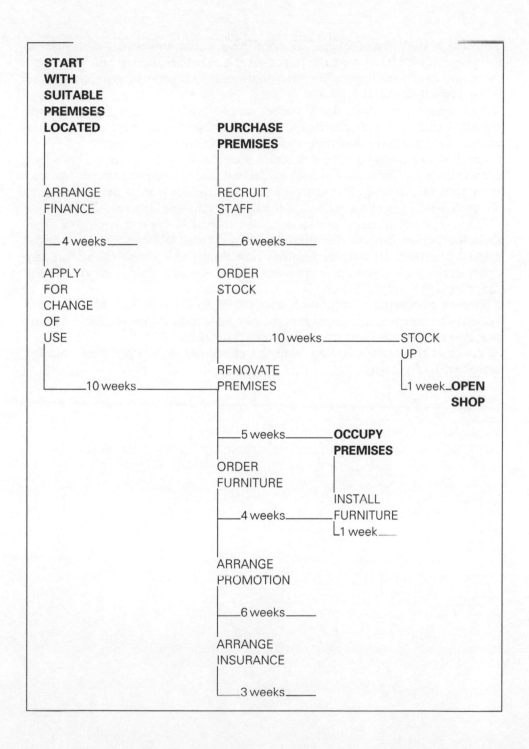

**START
WITH
SUITABLE
PREMISES
LOCATED**

ARRANGE
FINANCE

——4 weeks——

APPLY
FOR
CHANGE
OF
USE

————10 weeks————

**PURCHASE
PREMISES**

RECRUIT
STAFF

——6 weeks——

ORDER
STOCK

————10 weeks————

RENOVATE
PREMISES

——5 weeks——

ORDER
FURNITURE

——4 weeks——

ARRANGE
PROMOTION

——6 weeks——

ARRANGE
INSURANCE

——3 weeks——

STOCK
UP

L1 week—**OPEN
SHOP**

**OCCUPY
PREMISES**

INSTALL
FURNITURE
L1 week——

You will notice, in heavy type, some of the key decision points in the chart: the point at which you actually purchase the premises, occupy the shop and open the shop respectively. In each case there are actions which precede these key decision points.

You cannot purchase the premises until you have cleared the finance required and obtained permission to use the shop for your purpose. As you can see, we have estimated that obtaining permission takes longer.

Once the purchase has been secured many other actions can be initiated: recruitment of staff, renovation, ordering stock, ordering furniture and arranging advertising. Furniture cannot be installed until the building is ready. Stock cannot be installed on the shelves and displayed until it arrives.

Look on each of these various activities as 'paths' towards your goal. You cannot get there any quicker than the longest path! We call this the 'critical path' because it not only determines how long the exercise takes, but any delay in *this* path slows up the process, whereas minor delays in other paths may not make any difference.

Draw up a simple 'critical path analysis' chart for your own plans so that you may be able to make decisions and take actions in the most effective manner, and concentrate your energies on the critical areas.

You can then take the data from the chart and draw up a timetable for action with target dates.

Chapter 22

CHECK FOR VIABILITY

OBJECTIVE: to assess the plan that you have written and check that it is viable.

■ **Are you and your people up to it?**

■ **Are you sure you have a market for your goods and services?**

■ **Are you confident that you can manage the money side?**

■ **Have you taken full account of all other factors?**

The viability of your business plan depends crucially on:

• The men and women who will put it into effect
• The market for your goods and services
• The management of money

Some of these questions were mentioned in Chapter 4, but this is a more complete list for you to tackle now that you have completed your plans.

Men and women involved

• Do you and your management team have the motivation to see you through the hard times, the long hours and the frustrations of running this business?
• Do you and your management team have the technical skills to make the products and to provide the services you envisage?
• Do you and your management team have all the skills needed to look after the administrative side of the business, including all the money matters?
• Has your organization the ability to sell your goods or services to the potential customers you have identified?

- Are you prepared to modify your business plans in the light of what people will want to buy?
- Are you confident that you and your key managers will be able to manage skills and time to full effect?
- Have you made arrangements to plug any gaps in the expertise of your team? How do you plan to ensure that they are kept up to date?
- Will you be able to get all the skilled workers you need in the location(s) you have chosen for your business?
- Are working conditions, wages and other rewards adequate to attract and retain the staff you will need?
- Is there adequate transport available to enable your workforce to attend work regularly and punctually?
- Are there any special requirements related to qualified people (for example, divers, HGV drivers, transport managers, registered traders) in your business, and are you sure you can attract and retain such people?
- Have you decided what arrangements to make, if any, concerning pensions for your staff?

The market

- What is so special about the products that you intend to sell or the services that you intend to provide?
- How do you know that anyone will want to buy them?
- How much will you charge for your products or services? Will people be prepared to pay those prices?
- Are you sure that you can provide those goods or services at these prices, make a profit and manage cash flow?
- Why should anyone buy your goods or services rather than others on the market?
- Is this the right time to start providing the goods or services that you have in mind? Is this the moment when people will want them?
- Will you be able to develop your products or develop new products as your market develops?
- Have you considered how you will advertise or promote your products and how much this will cost?
- Do you know who your competitors are and what products they are selling?
- Have you spoken to any potential customers about the products or services that you intend to provide?
- Have you planned to make adequate provision for the follow-up of all enquiries from potential customers?

- Have you planned to institute a method of keeping abreast of the needs of your customers and the situation in the market-place?
- If you intend to use intermediaries (for example, wholesalers, distributors or agents), are you confident that they will promote your products and services?

Money management

- Will your business make a profit?
- Will you be able to pay each bill as it arrives?
- What financial resources will you need to enable you to be successful, especially over the initial trading period?
- Are you fully prepared to put up your share of this financial commitment?
- Do you need – can you obtain – a loan at a reasonable rate of interest?
- Are you confident that you can pay back any loans over a reasonable period, and pay the interest?
- Have you researched, listed and costed the expenditures that you will incur, and when these expenditures will be incurred?
- In particular, have you adequately researched your capital requirements and needs for 'working capital'?
- Have you a clear idea of when income will start to flow?
- Have you considered your insurance needs and any licences and permits that will be required?
- What sources of information, help and advice do you need? Do you know where these can be obtained?
- Have you discovered any problems that you have never had to deal with before?
- Have you made adequate provision for depreciation and for the rapid obsolescence of some kinds of equipment?
- Have you taken into account the sudden and dramatic rise in rent that might occur at the time of rent review?
- Have you built a sound relationship with your accountant and bank manager?

Other factors

- Are your chosen locations and buildings suitable for your purpose?
- Do your premises have all the services you require, including any special drainage, air extraction or high voltages?
- Are your facilities for manufacture, storage, sales and offices adequate?

- Will your suppliers, customers and delivery vehicles be able to get into and out of your premises, and manoeuvre adequately?
- Are you confident that you have made adequate arrangements for the maintenance of any crucial plant and equipment?
- Are you sure that you can obtain adequate supplies of raw materials from reliable sources?
- Can you get planning permission as required?

Chapter 23

IMPLEMENT

OBJECTIVE: to take action to implement the business plan.

- **Form an 'implementation group'**

- **Allocate responsibilities, set targets with performance indicators**

- **Monitor and discuss progress in your group**

- **Prepare to cope with change constructively**

As we have noted, the effective implementation of your plan requires action by a number of people, and the support of a number of people. In Chapter 3 we spoke of enlisting support for the production of the plan. It becomes even more important to consider the people who are involved now in its implementation.

IMPLEMENTATION GROUP

You will need to bring together the managers concerned: any who have not been involved in the build-up to the plan must now be taken through the main points and the implications for their particular departments.

For each area of the business clear goals need to be set, based on the plan, with a requirement to report back to the group on progress from time to time. The plan provides the basis for reporting back against unequivocal performance indices: for example, for sales, income and expenditure, advertising and promotion activities, manufacturing targets, quality factors, and so forth.

Many firms find it useful to prepare a monthly summary of the key performance indicators, say, within a week or so of the end of the month, and this data provides a sensible basis for reviewing progress and planning for the short term.

If each department has its own budget, with carefully selected subheads of expenditure, the monthly results can be shown against the anticipated figures, with a running total alongside.

Most companies find that such review meetings should be held at least once a month; probably once a week at the outset. There should be a clear agenda and a business-like discussion of the key performance indices.

COPING WITH CHANGE

Inevitably there will be deviations from the plan: sales are lower than expected, or higher; raw materials become expensive; a new competitor appears on the horizon.

Clearly one cannot just grind on as if nothing has happened. You will need to revise the plan, in particular, your sales projections, cashflow predictions and profit forecasts. In the light of these figures and your knowledge of the business, you must decide on what action to take.

If you have a computer with a spreadsheet, it takes only moments to estimate the effect of different scenarios when the basic business data is recorded on file; but the sums may take longer by hand.

There is always a temptation, when faced with adverse trading conditions, to attack expenditure, to reduce costs and to draw back. Before reacting in this way it is worth examining the figures and the situation carefully. Are there possibilities of sales in some areas or lines, even if not in others? Can you change track quickly to take advantage of changes in the market-place? Cutting costs is not always the best way.

Your detailed knowledge of the business, the environment and the market-place (if you have done your homework properly) should help you to make constructive decisions at such a time.

Chapter 24

UPDATING THE PLAN

> **OBJECTIVE: to decide on the optimum intervals at which to update the plan and how this should be done.**

- **Short-term problems may require revisions**

- **A year-end review of results will help you to plan for the future**

- **The discipline of zero-based budgeting has its place**

- **Scanning the environment and the market must not be neglected**

This book has been concerned with helping you to prepare a three-year business plan for your firm, with a specified starting date. The plan is comparatively detailed for the first year and less so for the second and third years.

Short-term problems
You may find that some factor deflects you from carrying out the plan as you had envisaged during the first year. In the light of the new situation, revise your existing data and use this to review the plan and make any necessary changes.

Rolling forward
Failing this, assuming that the deviations are not too large, you should be in a position towards the end of the first year to take stock of the company position, note where you had under- or over-estimated and to understand why this happened.

Your next step is to 'roll the plan forward'. By this we mean taking the second year of your original plan and making it the first year of a new business plan. In the light of your experience you should be able to plan more accurately than before.

Once again, prepare a month-by-month plan for the first year of the new plan, and quarterly for a further two years.

Zero based budget

You will need to make due allowances for inflation, but do not make the mistake of simply adding another ten per cent to everything and calling this a revised plan.

Take each item, one by one, and consider what adjustments to make. In some cases it will be quite satisfactory to take last year's figure and to add some. But if you do this for all items, the business will, over the years, start to build 'fat' into the system.

Going back to basics and working out what each item should cost, or what price should be charged from first principles (what we call 'zero-based budgeting') is a healthy exercise that should not be shirked.

Scanning

The environmental scan (Chapter 7) and the market scan (Chapter 6) should also be repeated at decent intervals, say, once a year. Although one can get useful information from salespeople and senior managers if they keep their ears to the ground, this data is not 100 per cent reliable. If you are in receipt of public funds make an effort to keep in touch with the appropriate officials in the funding body. React to their concerns in a constructive manner.

Such scanning will inform your decisions for the updated plan.

Above all, *keep close to your customers*.

Part Seven

THE BUSINESS PLAN

This part contains an outline of a 'blank' business plan which can be copied and completed to form a presentation of your business plan. However, each business has its own characteristics and you may have to modify this plan to suit your own particular business.

You may wish to add a quarterly summary of balance sheet movements as described in Chapter 17, or a quarterly schedule of assets by category as described in Chapter 14. If you consider the document is becoming too cumbersome it may be helpful to present some tables in appendices, for example, the sales and revenue forecasts, profit and loss forecasts, cash flow forecasts and balance sheets.

Business Plan

_____

(name of business)

_____

_____

(address of business)

Nature of the Business

(A description of the nature of the products and services to be provided and an outline of the customers and mode of promotion and delivery)

Key People

(The names of the key people who will work in the business and an outline of the knowledge, skills and experience they will contribute to the success of the enterprise. Also, an indication of staff recruitment – how many and with what skills)

(Areas of skill and knowledge which are needed in addition to those mentioned above and how these will be dealt with)

Sales Plan

CUSTOMERS
(A precise description of the key decision-makers involved in purchasing the products and services)

PATTERN OF DEMAND
(An outline of anticipated sales over the first year, including any anticipated seasonal variation in sales)

Sales Plan – Continued

PRICING POLICY
(An outline of the prices to be charged and how these were determined)

REACHING CUSTOMERS
(An outline of how potential customers will be informed about the products and services, attracted to make enquiries, and encouraged to make purchases)

Sales and Revenue Forecast

Month	1	2	3	4	5	6	7	8	9	10	11	12	TOTAL

SALES

Number of Units A
(price of A)
Income from A

Number of Units B
(price of B)
Income from B

Number of Units C
(price of C)
Income from C

Gross Income

RECEIPTS

Cash Sales

Credit Sales

TOTAL SALES

RECEIPTS

Profit and Loss Forecast

	Year I	Year 2	Year 3
SALES FORECAST: units sold	_____	_____	_____
@ price per unit of P1 . . .			
GROSS TURNOVER (quantity x price)	_____	_____	_____
Less: Variable costs	_____	_____	_____
Gives GROSS PROFIT	_____	_____	_____
Plus other business income	_____	_____	_____
TOTAL INCOME	_____	_____	_____
Less: OVERHEADS from			
BELOW	_____	_____	_____
PROFIT/(LOSS)			
(before tax)	_____	_____	_____

OVERHEADS

	Year I	Year 2	Year 3
Employees' wages	_____	_____	_____
Employers' National Insurance	_____	_____	_____
Training of staff	_____	_____	_____
Rent (rented premises)	_____	_____	_____
Rates and water rates	_____	_____	_____
Fuel (gas, electricity, etc.)	_____	_____	_____
Telecommunications	_____	_____	_____
Computer running costs	_____	_____	_____
Postage	_____	_____	_____
Printing and stationery	_____	_____	_____
Subscriptions and periodicals	_____	_____	_____
Advertising and promotions	_____	_____	_____
Repairs and maintenance	_____	_____	_____
Insurances	_____	_____	_____
Professional fees	_____	_____	_____
Interest payments	_____	_____	_____
Bank charges	_____	_____	_____
Vehicle and travel costs			
(other than depreciation)	_____	_____	_____
Depreciation – vehicle	_____	_____	_____
Depreciation – other assets	_____	_____	_____
Other expenses (specify)	_____	_____	_____
TOTAL OVERHEADS	_____	_____	_____

Note: tax on profit will be deducted according to the Inland Revenue rules.

Cash Flow Forecast (First Year)

MONTH	0	1	2	3	4	5	6	7	8	9	10	11	12	TOTAL

RECEIPTS

OPENING BALANCE (B)

Owners' investment
Loans from . . .
Cash sales
Credit sales
Asset disposals
Interest received

TOTAL RECEIPTS (R)

PAYMENTS

Premium on lease
Purchase of property
Purchase of plant,
 furniture and fittings

Purchase of vehicles
Raw materials
Goods for sale
Employees' net wages
Income tax and NI
Training expenses

Rent (rented premises)
Rates and water rates
Fuel (gas, electricity, etc.)
Telecommunications
Computer running costs
Postage

Printing and stationery
Subscriptions and periodicals
Advertising and promotions
Repairs and maintenance
Vehicle and travel costs
 (exclude vehicle purchases)

Insurances
Professional fees
Loan repayments
Bank charges
Bank interest
Value Added Tax
Other expenses (specify)

TOTAL PAYMENTS (P)

RECEIPTS LESS PAYMENTS
FOR THE MONTH (M)

**CASH REMAINING IN
THE BUSINESS (C)**

Cash Flow Forecast (Years 2 and 3)

YEAR/QUARTER	2/1	2/2	2/3	2/4	3/1	3/2	3/3	3/4
RECEIPTS								
OPENING BALANCE (B)								
Owners' investment								
Loans from . . .								
Cash sales								
Credit sales								
Asset disposals								
Interest received								
TOTAL RECEIPTS (R)								
PAYMENTS								
Premium on lease								
Purchase of property								
Purchase of plant, furniture and fittings								
Purchase of vehicles								
Raw materials								
Goods for sale								
Employees' net wages								
Income tax and NI								
Training expenses								
Rent (rented premises)								
Rates and water rates								
Fuel (gas, electricity, etc.)								
Telecommunications								
Computer running costs								
Postage								
Printing and stationery								
Subscriptions and periodicals								
Advertising and promotions								
Repairs and maintenance								
Vehicle and travel costs (exclude vehicle purchases)								
Insurances								
Professional fees								
Loan repayments								
Bank charges								
Bank interest								
Value Added Tax								
Other expenses (specify)								
TOTAL PAYMENTS (P)								
RECEIPTS LESS PAYMENTS FOR THE MONTH (M)								
CASH REMAINING IN THE BUSINESS (C)								

Capital Expenditure

(A list of all the capital items (including buildings and vehicles) costing more than £250 required in the first three years, including an indication in each case as to whether the article will be purchased outright or subject to a loan, rented or leased)

CAPITAL ITEM	INITIAL COST	ANTICIPATED PURCHASE DATE	METHOD OF PAYMENT	COMPLETION OF LOAN OR END OF LEASE

Stock Levels

RAW MATERIALS

ITEM	STOCK LEVELS (minimum)		STOCK LEVELS (average)		RE ORDER		
	Quantity	Value (£)	Quantity	Value (£)	Frequency	Quantity	Value (£)

TOTAL AVERAGE VALUE OF RAW MATERIAL STOCKS HELD £_____

WORK IN PROGRESS

ITEM	STOCK LEVELS (minimum)		STOCK LEVELS (average)	
	Quantity	Value (£)	Quantity	Value (£)

TOTAL AVERAGE VALUE OF WORK IN PROGRESS HELD £_____

FINISHED GOODS

ITEM	STOCK LEVELS (minimum)		STOCK LEVELS (average)		RE-ORDER (if this is appropriate)		
	Quantity	Value (£)	Quantity	Value (£)	Frequency	Quantity	Value (£)

TOTAL AVERAGE VALUE OF FINISHED GOODS STOCKS HELD £_____

Financial Base

(How the company will be funded, including any loans or overdrafts that may be required)

Management Information Systems

(An outline of how financial and other quantitative records will be maintained)

Opening Balance Sheet
(Commencement of year)

LIABILITIES	ASSETS
Capital (owners' money)	**Fixed assets**
Owners' investment Retained profit	Buildings Plant Furniture Vehicles Computers
	_____
Deferred liability	**Current assets**
Term loan _____	Raw materials Finished goods Debtors Cash
	_____
Current liabilities	
Creditors Tax liability Bank overdraft	

Closing Balance Sheet
(end of the year)

LIABILITIES	ASSETS
Capital (owners' money)	**Fixed assets**
Owners' investment Retained profit	Buildings Plant Furniture Vehicles Computers
_____	_____
Deferred liability	**Current assets**
Term loan _____	Raw materials Finished goods Debtors Cash
	_____
Current liabilities	
Creditors Tax liability Bank overdraft	
_____	_____
_____	_____

Special Factors and Risk Assessment

Action Plan

(The dates intended for fresh initiatives to be taken based on the plan; the key decisions/actions that need to be taken; and any instance where more information is required and how this will be obtained)

DECISION/ ACTION	TARGET DATE	INFORMATION NEEDED?

INDEX